Louis L'Amour's sagas were *not* why we had made sure our girls were actively involved in a strong church, youth groups, and Bible studies, *not* why we had made sure we started each and every day of their lives at home with time in God's Word and prayer.

Well, I want to pass on to you some wisdom my wiser and more seasoned friend gave me. She simply asked, "Liz, what are you doing to remedy the situation?"

You can be sure when Jim got home that evening, I shared her probing question with him. What *were* we doing to remedy the situation? Nothing!

"What *could* we do?" became our passionate prayer concern.

Soon these "concerns" led us to call Courtney and offer her our credit card number and the gift of $25 each month for books to be chosen from a Christian book catalog. (Oh, yes—Paul was to select $25 worth of books for himself, too!) Just because there were no Christian libraries on Kauai, and just because there were few Christian books in the public libraries, didn't mean that we couldn't help put edifying Christian works into their home and hands and hearts!

And so Courtney began to "feed" on something of substance.

Soon a letter arrived from Courtney telling me that her first selection was a three-pack of biographies on the lives of Fanny Crosby, Dorothy Carey, and Susanna Wesley.

Next a call came saying, "Oh, Mom, I can't wait to discuss Dorothy Carey's life with you!"

Then another note—"Mom, this seemed like something you could share with your ladies when you teach." It was an excerpt from a letter written by Susanna Wesley to her famous son, John, the founder of Methodism:

> I will tell you what rule I observed... when I was young, and too much addicted to childish diversions, which was this— Never to spend more time in mere recreation in one day than I spend in private religious devotions.[2]

Quickly I prayed, "Oh, thank You, Lord! Now *this* is more like it! And thank You, too, Lord, for Courtney's encouraging message to me from this wonderful book about a woman who loved You too!"

(And, by the way, reading the inspiring story of Fanny Crosby's life next led Courtney to order several volumes on the great hymns of the Christian faith and how they came to be written.)

My friend, is there a situation you need to "remedy"? Are you feeding on foolishness or rooting through ashes or merely sniffing the wind? God—*Jehovah-Rohi*—tells us to beware of the inevitable stumbling and falling that is sure to result! At the same time, He invites us into the safety and shelter of His promised care, the care of *Jehovah-Rohi,* the One who promises to feed and to lead us.

*This
book belongs to*

_____

*...a woman who delights
in God's promises.*

Do you want to be safe from the influence, ways, and lusts of the world and the flesh (1 John 2:16)? From the sin which so easily entangles us (Hebrews 12:1)? Then, dear one, delight yourself in the Lord, in His provision, in His Word. Faithfully feed on the things which possess true substance and real meaning. When we remember that "all Scripture is given by inspiration by God and is profitable" (2 Timothy 3:16) and partake of such divine substance, then we are fed, we are led...*and* we are safe!

## ~ *Reflecting Again on God's Promises* ~

Just imagine! As one of God's precious sheep you are cherished and cared for by the Shepherd! By penning these two Hebrew words—*Jehovah-Rohi*—which translates *the-LORD-is-my-shepherd,* David's imagery lifts our thoughts to the highest and tenderest aspect of God's nature. No other name of God carries with it the intimacy and tender friendship of *Jehovah-Rohi.* Yes, you and I are cared for and cherished—so much so that God promises to lead us and feed us. Think of it! To be the friend of God!

The Lord is your Shepherd, precious one, and He will take care of you. It's a promise!

# ~2~

# God's Promise
# of Provision

~

*I shall not want.*
PSALM 23:1

*And my God
shall supply all your need
according to His riches
in glory by Christ Jesus.*
PHILIPPIANS 4:19

~

Step up to your impossible situation…
and step out in faith.
God not only leads you and cares for you,
but He provides for you, too.
Where God guides, He provides.
Therefore, you shall not want…for anything!
—*Elizabeth George*

*Y*2K.

Perhaps you remember Y2K, the catchphrase that was coined to mark mankind's entry into the twenty-first century, into the year 2000. Originally meant to serve as an advance warning to prepare computers and business systems for new dating, one of Y2K's side effects was rising fear around the globe.

Normally level-headed people sold off their stocks.

General purchases dropped as folks curtailed spending... while gun sales rose.

Even Christians (who have the Lord, *Jehovah-Rohi*, as their Shepherd) stockpiled food, hoarded cash, stored food and water in church basements, cancelled Christmas, postponed important decisions, and refused to make commitments into the year 2000.

And it's also interesting to note that Christian book sales on subjects like prayer and the promises of God were up.[1]

People definitely geared up for hardship.

Hardship, however, is not unique to the new millennium. Hardship has touched mankind throughout time. The Bible and history books are filled with records of economic depression, social oppression, wars, famines, and disasters. Suffering has been a fact of life since Adam and Eve disobeyed God (Genesis 3). And because of these realities, it's easy to understand why we're so tempted to look down through the corridors of time-future and succumb to anxiety, worry, fear, and hopelessness. We just don't see how we're going to make it!

But, dear one, our wonderful God has already looked down through the corridors of time-future...*and* time-eternal. (Indeed, they are *His* corridors!) He already knows His full-scale plan for mankind. And He already knows His personal plan for you and for each of His children. You see, He alone is the one who knows the end from the beginning (Isaiah 46:10).

When David, the sweet singer of Israel, penned Psalm 23, a psalm and song of praise about God, about our amazing Shepherd, he wrote...

> *The LORD is my shepherd; I shall not want.*

We learned in the last chapter that "the LORD is my shepherd" is actually a name of God, *Jehovah-Rohi*. But God has other names. And the fact that David could say "I shall not want" reminds us of yet another name of God—*Jehovah-Jireh*—and another characteristic of God—His provision.

When these two aspects of God's character—*Jehovah-Rohi* and *Jehovah-Jireh*—are put together, they convey oh so clearly to us that God not only leads us and cares for us, but He provides for us, too. In other words, where God guides, He provides. Therefore, we shall not want...for anything!

# *Meet Jehovah-Jireh*

But what does *Jehovah-Jireh* mean...and mean to you and me?

Most of the compound names of God spring from a specific historic incident, and we first meet *Jehovah-Jireh* in Genesis 22. Here we see Him providing for His faithful patriarch, Abraham, and Abraham's son Isaac. Let's watch the scene unfold.

- ❧ *Abraham's command*—came out of heaven from God Himself: "Take now your son, your only son Isaac, whom you love, and go to the land of Moriah, and offer him there as a burnt offering..." (verses 1,2).

- ❧ *Abraham's response*—was immediate obedience: "So Abraham rose early in the morning...and took...Isaac his son...and went to the place of which God had told him" (verse 3), a place that was about a 60-mile trek.

- ❧ *Abraham's son*—Isaac had a question: As they walked along with the wood, the fire, and the knife necessary to slay an animal sacrifice, Isaac asked, "...where is the lamb for a burnt offering?" (verse 7).

- ❧ *Abraham's answer*—revealed his trust in the Lord: "My son, God will provide [*Jehovah-Jireh*] for Himself the lamb for a burnt offering" (verse 8).

Exactly how did *Jehovah-Jireh* provide?

Arriving at the place of sacrifice, faithful (and trembling?) Abraham bound Isaac with rope, laid him on an altar, and took out his knife to slay his only son. As Abraham prepared to follow through on God's command to offer his son as a sacrifice, the Angel of the Lord called out from heaven, "Do not lay your hand on the lad, or do anything to him; for now I know that you fear God, since you have not withheld your son, your only son, from Me" (verse 12).

And do you know what happened next? God, *Jehovah-Jireh*, provided a lamb for the sacrifice. As Abraham looked up, he spotted a ram caught in the bushes, a ram which he used in Isaac's place for the burnt offering.

No wonder Abraham named the place "The-Lord-Will-Provide"! "In the Mount of the LORD it shall be provided" (verse 14).

∽ ✻ ∽

## ∽ *Reflecting on God's Promises* ∽

Do you ever feel overwhelmed by something you've been asked to do or something that is expected of you...and you just can't see *how* you can do it?

I know that so many of the women I talk to feel overcome by their roles (wife, mother, daughter, grandmother), their responsibilities (at home, in the neighborhood, at school, at church, and even on the job), and the challenge of just keeping up their health and personal grooming!

But Abraham shows us the way:

He responded immediately to the call
    of God,
He moved out in obedience, and
He trusted the Lord.

And...on the other side of his faith, his responding-moving-out-and-trusting actions, was God's provision.

That's how it must be with us, too, dear one. We have our "commands," our responsibilities, spelled out in God's Word. And, of course, we must prioritize and plan and prepare and pray about the wisest ways to follow through and fulfill God's commands.

Then the moment comes when we must move out. Action must be taken, whether we think we can "make it" or not. Whether what God is asking of us makes sense or not. Whether it seems do-able or not. Whether it feels good or not.

Yes, faith must finally take a step!

The Red Sea didn't part until Moses lifted his hand and his rod (Exodus14:16,21).

The waters of the Jordan didn't divide until the priests stepped into them (Joshua 3:13).

Rahab's family wasn't saved until she tied a scarlet thread in her window (Joshua 2:21).

The widow's oil didn't increase until she poured it out (2 Kings 4:5).

Naaman's leprosy wasn't cured until he washed in the Jordan River (2 Kings 5:14).

In every one of these situations (and there are many more in the Bible) the miracle occurred *after* faith acted. And in every case the predicament was impossible! Absurd! And in every case God pressed His dear children right up to the edge...until common sense and reason had to be abandoned and faith was forced to bloom, until the "seen" had to be replaced with faith that is "unseen."

So, dear one, step up to your impossible situation...and step out in faith. Determine to do what God is asking of you...and act on His command. Then you will know God's provision.

~ ~ ~ ~ ~ ❧ ~ ~ ~ ~ ~

## God Provides

*Jehovah-Jireh.* How reassuring to know that God sees our needs and provides for them.

But how do we know that God will provide? We have the *promise* of God (which requires it), but we also have the very nature of the *Person* of God (which demands it). He is all-knowing. He is all-wise. And He is all-powerful. With God, to see is also to provide. Or, put another way,

In His omniscience (His complete knowledge), God *knows* (or sees) our need;
In His power, He *can* provide; and
In His goodness, He *must* provide for what His knowledge and wisdom reveal to be the true needs of His people.

Think a little further. For God to see a need in His child and *not* meet that need would be evil, and God, by His very nature, cannot even conceive of evil (James 1:13). Therefore, with God, pre-vision and pro-vision are one and the same. When His pre-vision sees a need, His pro-vision meets it!

∾ ✤ ∾

## ∾ *Reflecting on God's Promises* ∾

I just paused to make a list of life's needs, and I came up with a needs-list that I believe fits for most of us women.

First and foremost, there's the physical area of everyday life, the need you and I have for food and clothing. And yet we know that God's Word tells us not to worry about our life—about what we'll eat or drink or wear (Matthew 6:25).

Why? Because God feeds the birds of the air, and He'll also feed us (verse 26). And God clothes the lilies of the field, and He'll also clothe us (verse 28).

The Bible also describes God's amazing (and miraculous!) provision for the Israelites as they wandered for 40 years in the wilderness. As the people in Nehemiah's day affirmed,

> You also gave Your good Spirit to instruct them, and did not withhold Your manna from their mouth, and gave them water for their thirst. Forty years You sustained them in the wilderness, so that they lacked nothing: Their clothes did not wear out and their feet did not swell (Nehemiah 9:20,21).

God, *Jehovah-Jireh*, provided guidance, food, water, clothes, and health for His people—all that they needed—and He did it for 40 years!

Now, *that's* provision! And, marvel of marvels, "they lacked nothing" (which is the same picture we have in Psalm 23:1—*"I shall not want"*). That's our God, *Jehovah-Jireh!*

Then there's our need for the less measurable things of life—for leadership, for comfort, for instruction, for encouragement, for protection, for love, for safety, for purpose, for belonging and fellowship and friendship. What a sweet thought to realize that we can count on *Jehovah-Jireh's* promise to provide for them, too!

Later in Psalm 23, we'll see God meet each and every one of life's requirements, but for now enjoy these reflections about God's provision from Dr. Harry Ironside, former pastor of the famed Moody Memorial Church in Chicago. He wrote of God and His promises, "I shall not want...

...rest, for He maketh me to lie down.

...refreshment, for He leadeth me beside the still waters.

...restoration, for He restoreth my soul.

...guidance, for He leadeth me in the paths of righteousness.

...confidence, for I will fear no evil.

...companionship, for Thou art with me.

...comfort, for Thy rod and Thy staff, they comfort me.

...provision, for Thou preparest a table.

...joy, for my cup runneth over.

...anything in this life, for goodness and mercy
shall follow me all the days of my life.
...anything in eternity, for I will dwell in the
house of the Lord forever."[2]

"I shall not want." These words of promise,
dear one, should translate in our hearts and
minds to "I shall not fear"! Truly, God promises
to provide our every need, both present and
future!

## God's Provision Is Seen

Just one more thought as we consider God's provision.

Do you remember how Abraham answered Isaac's question regarding the lamb for the sacrifice? He said, "My son, God will provide [*Jehovah-Jireh*] for Himself the lamb for a burnt offering" (Genesis 22:8). This is the same as Abraham's saying "God's provision shall be seen" (verse 14).

And it was! Right there on Mount Moriah, the place where God instructed Abraham to sacrifice his son, *Jehovah-Jireh's* provision was seen in the ram caught in the bushes. As one Bible version translates Genesis 22:14, "God will see to it."[3]

What a wonderful wealth we have in the character of God that His title *Jehovah-Jireh* denotes! Our Shepherd *sees* our needs and *sees to* our needs. And when we *see* His provision, we need to *see to it* that He is greatly praised!

## ∼ *Reflecting on God's Promises* ∼

Beloved, before we leave this marvelous revelation about our marvelous God, I want us to cherish the fullness of the meaning of *Jehovah-Jireh* from these other translations of Psalm 23:1, "The LORD is my Shepherd, I shall not want":

> The LORD is my shepherd, therefore, I can lack nothing.
> The LORD shepherds me, I shall never be in need.
> Jehovah is my shepherd, I lack nothing.
> The LORD takes care of me as His sheep; I will not be without any good thing.
> Because the LORD is my shepherd, I have everything I need![4]

The promises of Psalm 23, verse 1, should be life-changing truths for us. And we should deeply embed them into our soul and evidence a strong faith by counting on God's promised provision...for our every need...forever.

What the famous British preacher G. Campbell Morgan wrote of Psalm 23:1 is true: "This is not only the first statement of this song, it is its inclusive statement. Everything that follows [verse 1] interprets the glory and sufficiency of the fact [here] declared. When this is said...the LORD is my shepherd, I shall not want...all is said."[5]

# ~3~

# *God's Promise of Rest*

~

*He makes me to lie down in green pastures.*
Psalm 23:2

*Come to Me, all you who labor and are heavy laden,*
*and I will give you rest.*
*Take My yoke upon you and learn from Me,*
*for I am gentle and lowly in heart,*
*and you will find rest for your souls.*
Matthew 11:28-29

~

What happens when we
withdraw from the clamor of a sinful world and
enter into the serenity available in God's green pastures?
We experience the same sense of rejuvenation,
the same revival of spirit,
the same deep satisfaction that literal sheep enjoy
when resting in the presence of a faithful shepherd.
—*Elizabeth George*

$\mathcal{T}$his can't be Los Angeles!"

As I turned my car off the busy state highway in Simi Valley, California, and onto a narrow asphalt road lined for miles on both sides with graceful five-story-high eucalyptus trees set ten feet apart, I was amazed! Quickly civilization disappeared and I was alone in the beautiful, untouched foothills of the Santa Monica mountains. Eventually the rural drive led me to the old stone gatehouse of The Brandeis Institute, where I had a job interview with its executive director. I rang a bell and waited. Finally, the estate keeper arrived to let me through the gate. After another half-mile drive, I arrived at the century-old stone hunting lodge that housed the offices of The Institute.

I was back in time! Or was I in another country? I couldn't tell. But I liked what I saw and smelled and sensed. I could already feel myself relaxing even as I faced the stress of an interview. Tucked away from hectic freeways, tract homes, and strip malls, the quiet pastoral beauty of this undisturbed hill country was wonderfully peaceful.

Later, after I began working at The Institute, I learned the history of this restful place from the Israeli director, Dr. Shlomo Bardin. The Jewish community of Los Angeles had specifically selected this country site because it reminded them of their homeland in Israel. Its tranquil hills looked like those in the Judean hills of the Holy Land. The mountains, the climate, and the vegetation were the same, too. And so The Brandeis Institute was founded there on this remote acreage, a kibbutz-style retreat center was built, and the land was left unchanged. It was to this wonderful "home away from home" that these Jews came each Friday afternoon before sunset to withdraw from the mainstream, to reflect on their heritage, to worship, and to rest.

I have to admit that each Friday when I was sent away early before their worship began, I wished that I, too, could stay there and rest in this picturesque setting!

Ahhh, rest! Our bodies need it. Our souls crave it. And now, as we step into verse 2 of the Shepherd Psalm, we realize that rest is yet another of God's precious promises to us, His precious sheep. "He makes [us] to lie down in green pastures."

Let's see what God has in mind for our rest.

## The Place of Rest

First, there's a *place* God guides us to, a place of "green pastures." And what do you suppose is in those green pastures where the Shepherd will ensure that we lie down?

*Food.* Food is abundantly available in God's green pastures. That's the picture the psalmist is painting here with his descriptive language—a picture of abundance and luxury. And a good shepherd carefully picks a place of pastureland that's filled to overflowing with fresh, new, tender grass. His heart is set on finding a place containing plenty of delicate green grass that will provide nourishment, health, and fresh energy for his sheep.

*Rest.* Rest, too, would occur as the sheep lay down in green pastures. The scene is one of satisfaction and rest. Of calm and contentment. Of sheer enjoyment. Oh, would that grass ever be cool on a hot day in a dry desert climate, providing the perfect place of refreshment and rest for weary sheep!

∾ ⁂ ∾

## ∾ *Reflecting on God's Promises* ∾

Dear one, as sheep who belong to the Great Shepherd, we, too, can partake of green pastures. How? By having a "quiet time." We have all of the Shepherd and all of His Word available to us...if we will simply lie down in His green pastures and partake! All we need to do is stop everything and enjoy a time of resting and lingering with the Lord as we feed on His Word.

What happens when we withdraw from the clamor of a sinful world and enter into the serenity available in God's green pastures? We experience the same sense of rejuvenation, the same revival of spirit, the same deep satisfaction that literal sheep enjoy when resting in the presence of a faithful shepherd. Therefore we must always be checking up on ourselves about our time in God's Word, in His green pastures.

§ *Necessary*—Do you believe that time spent with God in the green pastures of His Word is an absolute necessity, just as food and rest are absolutely necessary for every sheep?

J. I. Packer, author of *Knowing God,* warns, "Disregard the study of [the Word] of God and you sentence yourself to stumble and blunder through life, blindfolded, as it were, with no sense of direction, and no understanding of what surrounds you."[1]

§ *Regular*—Is your time spent in the lush pastures of God's Word regular? Is it daily? When you think about how regularly and how often you eat physical food, how does your feeding on spiritual food measure up?

One evening, at a "roundtable" discussion held around our dining table, my husband, Jim, was sharing the tiny pamphlet *Seven Minutes with God*[2] with a group of men who were students at The Master's College. Jim had purchased a copy of this priceless booklet for each one of them and was walking them through its seven-minute format for daily devotions. As the young men began to squirm, finally one of them cleared his throat and said what the others were thinking: "But, Professor George, isn't seven minutes a day with God in a quiet time just a little... ah...er...*un*-spiritual?"

Ever the teacher, my wise husband answered this question with a question—"Well, let me ask you men: How many of you spent an hour this past week in devotions?" When only a very few raised their hands (and while the others looked down sheepishly at theirs!), Jim continued, "You see, seven minutes a day with God is better than no minutes a day with God...and seven minutes a day with God adds up to about an hour a week."

Do you need to begin feeding regularly on God's green pastures? (And always remember—a wee bite is better than no bite at all!)

§ *Increasing*—Is your time spent in the lush pastures of the Scriptures increasing? Of course Jim didn't mean that those in his Bible study group should *only* spend seven minutes each day with God for the rest of their lives! No, time in God's Word should be ever-increasing.

So do as writer Ruth Graham says, citing one of her favorite Bible translations—"indulge" yourself! Do whatever you have to do to make time in God's Word exciting and meaningful, but keep on willfully indulging yourself...and in increasing amounts.

Which of these stages best describes your recent times in God's Word? 1) *the cod liver oil stage*—you take it like medicine; 2) *the shredded wheat stage*—it's nourishing but dry; or 3) *the peaches and cream stage*—it's consumed with passion and pleasure.[3]

And what steps could you take to reach the peaches and cream stage? Oh, that we would acquire an insatiable appetite for rich fellowship with the Lord through His Word that nothing else would satisfy!

∾ ∾ ∾ ∾ ∾ ⚕ ∾ ∾ ∾ ∾ ∾

Aren't you glad that God provides a place—His green pastures—for us to rest in and feed in?

But there's more!

## The Plan for Rest

In addition to a *place* of rest, we can also rest in God's *plan*. In His wisdom He plans (and ensures!) that we "lie down." Digging a little deeper, we learn that the kind of "lying down" that the Shepherd has in mind is no little nervous pause. No, the idea expressed is one of s-t-r-e-t-c-h-i-n-g out, of lying full-out, of completely reclining. The vivid, sensual picture is one of enjoyment and contentment and satisfaction. You see, while lying down in this way, rest would occur. Relaxation and refreshment would take place.

I remember reading the story of Alexander Solzhenitsyn's days in a Russian prison. A part of his torture was not being allowed to rest or sit down or lie down for days on end. Instead he was worked around the clock. I remember, too, thinking as I read, "Now *that* would be the worst torture there is—to be utterly exhausted, literally dead on your feet, and unable to lie down, stretch out, rest, and recover!"

But as I studied this familiar old psalm, I learned a few interesting facts about why a sheep will not lie down.

*Reason #1—Fear.* A sheep that is afraid will not lie down and get the rest it needs. I read one example of a shepherd leading his flock to a small brook which had a bounty of grass on both sides. Yet the flock refused to lie down because a large dog was on the other side of the stream.

And even after the shepherd slung a stone and frightened the dog off, the sheep still wouldn't relax. What did it take to persuade the sheep to lie down? It took the shepherd walking ahead of them to the brook. It took the presence of the shepherd to dispel all fear.

∾ ℀ ∾

## ∾ *Reflecting on God's Promises* ∾

You and I have the presence of the Shepherd, too, dear one. Therefore, as the Scripture says, "fear not."

Fear not, for I am with you;
Be not dismayed, for I am your God.
I will strengthen you,
Yes, I will help you,
I will uphold you with
My righteous right hand.
(Isaiah 41:10)

Do not be afraid, nor be dismayed,
For the LORD your God is with you
wherever you go.
(Joshua 1:9)

Do not fear nor be afraid of them;
For the LORD your God, He is the One who
goes with you.
He will not leave you nor forsake you.
(Deuteronomy 31:6)

And He said, "My Presence will go with you,
And I will give you rest."
(Exodus 33:14)

With these powerful promises from God to strengthen us, there's hope and help for you and me to defeat panic or anxiety and to get relief from insomnia! If these are problems for you, memorize these verses. And trust in them. Put them to work for you. Then, when you lie down, you can rest in the presence of the Shepherd. And, when you rise up after rest, you can declare in chorus with David, "I lay down and slept; I awoke, for the LORD sustained me" (Psalm 3:5).

*Reason #2—Hunger.* It's a fact that a sheep that's hungry will not lie down and receive the rest it needs. Instead, it wanders about restlessly, frantically searching for food. Thus the discontented sheep adds lack of rest to its problem of lack of food, loses its vigor and vitality, and fails to thrive.

But, beloved, our Shepherd feeds His sheep. As *Jehovah-Jireh* ("I shall not want"), He makes sure our food is always available. All we have to do is decide to feed upon it...to the full!

## ❧ *Reflecting on God's Promises* ❧

My dear pastor's wife, knowing that I was teaching Psalm 23, hand-carried an invaluable volume on shepherding all the way back from New Zealand to California just for me! She had met the widow of the author, who was a shepherd, there in the green rolling hills of lush New Zealand. In his book, he shared this insight:

So many Christians attempt to satisfy their hunger...from an occasional few minutes' "feeding" from the pulpit, from a radio broadcast, or from a television message, while others seek to satisfy their needs from the odd old devotional book, or the occasional Christian programme. This is not enough...to sustain the needy soul on a daily basis.... God provides for us on a daily basis, but we must plan to partake of His provision on a daily basis.[4]

Are you following the Shepherd? Are you lying down in His green pastures? And are you feeding to your heart's content on His provision?

*Reason #3—Fighting.* A sheep that's involved in or even witnessing fighting also cannot lie down and receive the rest it needs. Battles between members of a flock rob all the sheep of the rest they need because, when any tension or uneasiness exists, the flock will refuse to lie down, relax, and rest.

## ∾ *Reflecting on God's Promises* ∾

Consider this—Many Christians are weary and worn, not because of intense conflict with the evil one, but because of arguments among themselves. It's frightening to realize the harm done to others when we argue and fight in our homes and in our churches.

The chief challenge to us is to be sure that we're not participating in this kind of fighting at home or church! You and I must be certain that we're not a source of tension for others.

And another thing—We can enjoy rest when we withdraw from the friction and the fodder of gossip produced by others. Why would we feed on such slop when we can feed on the beauty of the Lord and enjoy His holiness? As His darling sheep, we must look to Him (and not to "them") and go on about the business of our grand duty and our chief work of following the Shepherd.

~ ~ ~ ~ ~ ✦ ~ ~ ~ ~ ~

## *The Procedure for Rest*

So let's see now...

We have a *place* to sup with the Shepherd (His *green pastures*).

We have a *plan* for ensuring that we sup with Him (that we *lie down*).

And now we learn that our Lord has a *procedure* that guarantees our time with Him—He *makes* us lie down...even when we don't want to!

God's procedure of *making* us lie down is a call to trust Him. Why? Because He alone knows the future. Only He knows what lies ahead for us...around the next bend...over the next hill...on the other side of the green pastures. Will it be a long, steep climb? Will the path narrow as it leads us around a dangerous mountain? Will the trail take us into the valley of the shadow of death? Are we headed into a desert or a roaring storm?

The Shepherd knows the path.

But He also knows His sheep and what it takes to prepare us to walk along the way. And so the Shepherd *makes* us lie down to fortify us for the trek. He makes certain that we won't tire, that we're not at risk because of weariness, that we're invigorated from our pasture-time for any strenuous climb. With His eye on tomorrow, He who alone knows all our tomorrows, leads us today.

Do you know the result of our time spent in the hush of communion with the Shepherd and apart from the rush of the commonplace? As God's prophet Isaiah reports, "Those who wait on the LORD shall renew their strength; they shall mount up with wings like eagles, they shall run and not be weary, they shall walk and not faint" (Isaiah 40:31). Our Shepherd knows this. And so, all along life's way, He *makes* us lie down in green pastures.

～ ❧ ～

## ～ *Reflecting on God's Promises* ～

As I reflected on God's procedure of *making* us lie down in His green pastures, I thought of a number of ways that He accomplishes our rest. Illness, surgery, and convalescence afford us time with the Shepherd. So do pregnancy and childbirth. And exhaustion, too, will certainly place us in the grassy pastures of the Lord.

Still another category of time in God's pastures involves just plain ol' being passed over, overlooked for service and ministry. For me, our family's initial time in Singapore as missionaries was just such a time.

Why did our church choose to send my husband to serve in Singapore? Well, one very practical reason was Singapore's Changi Airport, which serves every Asian country. The plane carrying our little family of four had barely landed to deposit us before my Jim was back in the air, off to another country. In essence, Jim's ministry "took off" before we landed! He was invited to preach, to speak, to minister not only in the churches in Singapore, but also in neighboring countries.

But me? I sat...and sat...and sat some more. My phone was definitely *not* ringing!

"Why, Lord?" I prayed. "Why did I spend these past months preparing to serve You here? Why did I so carefully select resources and topics and teaching notes and messages for a ministry to women here?" On and on my "whys" for the Lord went.

But of course God knew! I can tell you *now* why my phone was amazingly silent. My all-knowing, all-wise Shepherd was making me lie down in green pastures. It was an enforced rest—one that accomplished much in the three months no one called.

Our family needed time to adjust to a new culture...to adjust to living in a climate near the equator...to adjust to a life of walking and busses and taxis—and no car!

I needed time to set up a home for my family...to learn to shop daily by foot in the Asian food markets...to prepare mysterious foods(!) in unusual ways.

My daughters Katherine and Courtney, then in sixth and fifth grades, needed time to transition into a new school setting.

And so we waited. Or rather, *I* waited!

Looking back to my three months of pasture-time there in Singapore, I thank God for *making* me rest from ministry as He supplied what my dear family needed. They needed me, they needed a home, and they needed an anchor of stability (me again!).

One other rarity that God gave me in that precious period of time was solitude. He gave me months of "quiet time" with Him. My empty calendar and silent phone and lack of friends opened up hours on end each and every day...with Him.

Waiting. Waiting is hard for us in our spoiled, instant-access society. But what happens, dear one, while you and I wait on the Lord in His green pastures?

⸎    *Waiting* creates an opportunity to learn to trust the Lord. We are forced to come to grips with the fact that He alone knows what He is doing.

§ *Waiting* causes us to grow in patience as we wait...and wait...and wait some more...until finally we are content just to be with the Lord.

§ *Waiting* in the presence of God encourages us to know Him in new ways as "waiting time" forces creative fellowship to occur.

§ *Waiting* energizes us for the walk (or race or battle!) ahead. God's prophet Elijah lay down in His green pastures and slept and ate and drank—and then went on in the strength of that pasture-time for 40 days and 40 nights (1 Kings 19:4-8).

Are you waiting, my friend? It will be helpful if you think of yourself in your waiting time as being like a ship in a lock. It's not that you *wouldn't* like to go forward—you just *can't!* Why? Because you're in the lock. Forward movement is impossible. But...*while* you are in the lock...*while* you're unable to move ahead... you're moving upward, upward, upward instead! It's the same for us. A time of waiting "locks" us into a life of study, a life of prayer, a life of lingering with the Shepherd, a life of preparation...until we rise up and move ahead again, having received from our time of rest all that we need for life's next challenge.

Welcome waiting! No matter how it looks or feels, our waiting times are God's green pastures—pastures for food, for coolness, for rest, for relaxation, for health, for preparation, for revival, for intimacy with the Lord.

~ ~ ~ ~ ~ ✗ ~ ~ ~ ~ ~

Aren't you glad that God has a *place* for you to rest, a *plan* for your rest, and a *procedure* that ensures that you do rest? As a variety of translations of this wonderful promise, when woven together, assure us, "He makes me lie down in green pastures—where He creates a resting-place for me to repose in, and there He shall feed me until I am satisfied."[5]

# ~ 4 ~

# God's Promise
# of Peace

~

*He leads me beside the still waters.*
PSALM 23:2

*Peace I leave with you, My peace I give to you;*
*not as the world gives do I give to you. Let not your heart*
*be troubled, neither let it be afraid.*
JOHN 14:27

~

Like a river glorious is God's perfect peace....
Not a surge of worry, not a shade of care,
Not a blast of hurry touch the spirit there.
Stayed upon Jehovah, hearts are fully blest—
Finding, as He promised, perfect peace and rest.
—*Frances R. Havergal*[1]

God, who gives us His peace, extends rest to the weary and
renewal to the exhausted. He wants our souls to be at
peace, and He promises to accomplish that peace.
—*Elizabeth George*

*D*o you have a favorite place? A special place that ministers to your soul? That sharpens your perspective? That stimulates you in fresh new ways?

Jim and I have found just such a place where we love to retreat. And one of the best features about "our place" is that we don't have to travel very far to reach it. It's just a pleasant 45-minute drive up the Pacific Coast from our home.

What's there that regularly draws us? Well, of course there's the expanse of the Pacific Ocean and its never-ceasing, ever-ebbing-and-flowing surf. We never fail to walk along its sandy shore!

Then, after our walk on the beach, there's the charming sidewalk café beside a large pool that's fed by the spill of a soothing waterfall where we like to share a snack. Oh yes—there's also a cascading fountain in the center of the veranda where we enjoy our sandwich and coffee.

One day while I was thinking about our place (actually yearning for another visit there...*soon!*), it struck me that *water* is the common denominator in all that Jim and I love to do and see there. Yes, it's the water. It lures us there. And once we're there, it calms us, inspires us, energizes us, and moves us to refocus on God's larger plans for us.

As you and I look today at yet another of God's many provisions for us as His dear sheep, we discover an image of water. And beside it, beloved, God promises we will find the much-yearned-for and much-needed peace of mind and heart we so long for as "He leads [us] beside the still waters" (Psalm 23:2).

## The Still Waters

Let's pretend that you are asked to fill out a survey for women. And let's make-believe that one of the questions is, "What causes you to seek peace?" How do you think you would answer?

As I was preparing to write this chapter, I went through this exercise myself. Here are some of the answers I came up with. Let's see how they match up with yours.

*Busyness* is #1 on my list! It seems like I do a lot of running here and there. There's always just one more errand to run, just one more minute needed in the kitchen, just one more meal to fix, just one more load of laundry to run, just one more phone call to make, just one more.... On and on my busyness list goes!

*Responsibility* is next. You know, all those duties that fall on our feminine shoulders? And the expectation—from ourselves and from others—that the things on our busyness list will be performed. These demands can become a heavy burden.

*Tension* showed up next on my list. Whenever something is wrong in a home or a relationship, the tension and uneasiness drains us.

# Powerful Promises for Every Woman

## Elizabeth George

HARVEST HOUSE™ PUBLISHERS

EUGENE, OREGON

*Cover by Terry Dugan Design, Minneapolis, Minnesota*

For additional practical help, you'll want to obtain the supplemental volume *Powerful Promises™ for Every Woman Growth and Study Guide.*

## POWERFUL PROMISES™ FOR EVERY WOMAN
(Formerly *The Lord Is My Shepherd*)
Copyright © 2000 by Elizabeth George
Published by Harvest House Publishers
Eugene, Oregon 97402

Library of Congress Cataloging-in-Publication Data

George, Elizabeth, 1944-
Powerful promises for every woman / Elizabeth George.
    p. cm.
Includes bibliographical references.
ISBN 0-7369-1041-7 (pbk.)
   1. Women—Religious life.   2. Bible O.T. Psalms XXIII—Criticism, interpretation, etc.
I. Title.
BV4527.G463 2003
242'.643—dc21                                                                    2002010025

**Printed in the United States of America.**

   03   04   05   06   07   08   09   / BP-MS /   10   9   8   7   6   5   4   3   2

*Thank you to Jim George,*
*my husband and friend,*
*for your assistance, suggestions, and*
*guidance throughout this project.*

# Contents

# *An Invitation to...*

### have your life changed forever

Are you like most women, who are in need of strength, guidance, peace, and hope as you make your way through life? Then rejoice! God has powerful promises just for you...and this book highlights 12 of those promises. Prepare your heart to discover life-changing truths...

- ❧ about the Person and character of God,

- ❧ about God's faithfulness to His own,

- ❧ about the 12 promises found in the beloved Psalm 23, and

- ❧ about the moment-by-moment application of these 12 promises to the issues—and trials!—of your daily life.

Truly, you and I are most blessed to possess the promises of God to see us through every day and every problem that will ever come our way!

I also invite you to take advantage of the supplemental *Powerful Promises™ for Every Woman Growth and Study Guide*. This helpful volume will propel you down the path toward a better understanding of God's complete provision for you. Its practical exercises are suitable for individual or group study and are for women of all ages, whether married or single.

May you find the following testimony given by King Solomon to be true for you as God's child—

> *There has not failed one word*
> *of all His good promise*
> (1 Kings 8:56).

# God's Promises for You

~

*He will feed His flock like a shepherd.*
ISAIAH 40:11

*I am the good shepherd.*
*The good shepherd gives His life for the sheep.*
JOHN 10:11

~

We can thank God, our Shepherd, that
His care is unceasing,
His love is unending,
His guidance is unfailing, and
His presence is everlasting.
—*Elizabeth George*

$\mathcal{W}$henever I think of Psalm 23, the Shepherd Psalm, I'm instantly transported back to a visit to Oklahoma. I was there because my 92-year-old father, the sole caretaker of my mother (who was 86, suffering from memory loss, and blind) had fallen off his ladder onto the concrete floor in the garage while putting away Christmas decorations in the attic. With my dad immobilized and recovering, my brothers and I were taking turns being with them to help.

One of my stints found my parents and me in the family room one quiet evening. Dad was watching a ball game on television, Mom was enjoying a snooze on the couch, and I was working at the breakfast table on my lectures on Psalm 23 for our women's Bible study at church. As I adjusted myself in the antique chair, its creaking woke my mother.

"What's that?!" she started.

"It's me, Mother."

"Who are you?"

"I'm Elizabeth Ann."

"What are you doing?"

"I'm studying Psalm 23."

"What's that?"

"It's the psalm that says, 'The Lord is my shepherd.'"

And then my dear, sweet, Alzheimer-suffering mother recited Psalm 23 in its entirety—and in perfect King James English!

> The LORD is my shepherd; I shall not want.
> He maketh me to lie down in green pastures;
> He leadeth me beside the still waters.
> He restoreth my soul;
> He leadeth me in the paths of righteousness
> for His name's sake.
> Yea, though I walk through the valley of the
> shadow of death, I will fear no evil;
> for thou art with me; thy rod and thy staff they
> comfort me.
> Thou preparest a table before me in the
> presence of mine enemies; thou anointest my
> head with oil; my cup runneth over.
> Surely goodness and mercy shall follow me all
> the days of my life; and I will dwell in the
> house of the LORD forever.

I was amazed! Picture my little mother (all 4'6" left of her), elderly (86 years old), startled out of sleep, disoriented, unable to see, and a victim of dementia; and yet, from her heart, deeply stored there from childhood days-gone-by, poured forth the elegant simplicity of the Shepherd Psalm.

Then, after quoting the beloved Twenty-third Psalm, Mom was able to, in full trust, put her head down and...go back to sleep.

Dear friend, what I witnessed with my mother demonstrated what the promises of Psalm 23 can mean to every woman in all the "seasons" of life. I know how I cherish the Twenty-third Psalm's simple-yet-all-encompassing truths. I also enjoyed sharing these same truths with my daughters when they were growing up. And I know how they now love passing them on to their little toddlers. And on that special evening with my sweet parents, I glimpsed what the knowledge of the Shepherd means to a soon-to-be citizen of heaven.

∾ ✳, ∾

## ∾ *Reflecting on God's Promises* ∾

May I pause here as we begin our walk together with the Shepherd and ask you where life finds you today? What "season" are you in?

§ *Spring*—Are you in the early beginnings of life? Are you tasting the joy of fresh starts and taking your first steps as a Christian?

§ *Summer*—Or have you progressed along the way with the Lord to the place of wisdom, of a blossoming knowledge of the One you walk with?

§ *Fall*—Or is yours a fast-paced, terrific season of tremendous fruit-bearing, of harvest, of reaping profusely from the benefits that come from a close, sustained walk with God over time?

§ *Winter*—Or are you experiencing endings that for the first time seem to have no new beginnings? Are you being pressed to adjust to a new path that leads in directions you did not anticipate or choose? Are you approaching the next bend in the path with some measure of fear?

As I write these words today, I seem to be walking through several seasons of life at the same time! In the winter of sorrows and losses, my dear dad died (and so did my husband's mother) and my mother is institutionalized, no longer recognizing me in any way. Yet in the spring of new beginnings, I welcomed my first two grandbabies, one month apart! And in between, I'm personally relishing a time of great productivity as I enjoy health and ample time to finally write to my heart's content.

But, just like you, my friend, I need God's promises for the seasons I'm presently experiencing as well as those I've already walked through...and those I have yet to brave. We can both thank God, our Shepherd, that His care is unceasing, His love is unending, His guidance is unfailing, and His presence is everlasting. We can thank Him, too, for the 12 promises from the Shepherd Psalm that will stand us well through all the seasons of life. As the Psalm's precious fourth verse promises, *He is with us,* dear one, through every day, o'er all the way.

You and I are truly blessed because we have the Lord—and His promises—as a shepherd for all seasons!

~ ~ ~ ~ ~ ❧ ~ ~ ~ ~ ~

## *The Psalmist's Seasons*

Have you ever wondered about the life and the "seasons" of the writer of Psalm 23? I have. I always check the back cover or flyleaf of any book for information "About the Author." You see, before I read any book, I want to know what qualifies that author to write on his subject. Well, that's what we want to know regarding this Psalm. Just who is the author, and what qualifies him to write it?

A biographical sketch of the life of David, the inspired writer of Psalm 23, reveals that David, the psalmist of Israel, not only knew the refreshing seasons of youth and maturity but also...

- ❧ *A season of rejection*...when expelled from his home and throne,

- ❧ *A season of fear*...when fleeing from the murderous King Saul,

- ❧ *A season of discouragement*...as an anointed king, yet a homeless fugitive,

- ❧ *A season of disappointment*...when God did not allow him to build the temple, and

§ *A season of heartbreak*...as he suffered the death of an infant son and witnessed strife and death among his children.

What's true in music is also true of David: On any stringed instrument, it's the strings that are strung the tightest that emit the sweetest music and play the sweetest songs. Yes, only someone who had experienced life and its hardships could have written the Twenty-third Psalm...

> For David's psalm had ne'er been sung
> If David's heart had ne'er been wrung.[1]

## *The Psalmist*

A quick look at David's life reveals many strengths and accomplishments. And the finest thing that can be said about David is that he was *a man of great faith.* David was not only an ancestor of Jesus Christ, but was also described by God Himself as "a man after My own heart, who will do all My will" (Acts 13:22). A thousand years later, David, the man of great faith, was honored with a listing in God's "Hall of Faith" in Hebrews 11.

Yet, just as a coin has two sides, so does the life of David. You see, he was also *a man of great failure,* a man who fell. Not only did David commit adultery with Bathsheba, but he also cold-bloodedly arranged for the murder of her husband (2 Samuel 11). Still another of David's failures was his directly disobeying God in taking a census of the people (2 Samuel 24).

# ∼ *Reflecting on God's Promises* ∼

As you and I walk through Psalm 23, we'll be stopping many times (as we are now) to consider the life lessons we can learn not only from the Shepherd and the Shepherd Psalm, but also from the life of David.

Our brief look at David, a man of faith and failure, offers specific instruction for us:

*Lesson #1—David admitted his failures.*

To the prophet Nathan, David confessed, "I have sinned against the LORD." Then we're told the good news that the Lord marvelously "put away" David's sin (2 Samuel 12:13). The Bible makes it wonderfully clear that "he who covers his sins will not prosper, but whoever confesses and forsakes them will have mercy" (Proverbs 28:13).

Are there any unconfessed sins in your life, dear friend? As the famous British preacher Charles H. Spurgeon once counseled, "Let us go to Calvary to learn how we may be forgiven." That's good advice for us as New Testament believers. At Calvary, at the cross of Jesus Christ, we learn that Jesus truly paid it all—the total penalty and price for our sins. Our responsibility is to confess those sins. His is to forgive. And, beloved, there is no sin too great to be forgiven!

And just one more thought: After David admitted his failure, the joy of his salvation was restored, and his sins were washed whiter than snow (see Psalm 51)! These same joys await you and me each and every time we acknowledge our transgressions.

*Lesson #2—David suffered sin's consequences.*

Although David was forgiven by God, he paid a price for his disobedience. A classic illustration teaches us a lesson on the consequences of sin: We can drive nails into a board, and we can remove the nails, but the nail holes—the scars—remain. David's life was indeed scarred by his sinful failures. His baby died, his son betrayed him, and his family was divided. Yes, David definitely suffered for his sin!

When I speak to groups of women, I often share the heartfelt words of two female authors I admire who take into consideration the reality of sin's consequences upon our lives. The first is Anne Ortlund, who writes: "In my heart I do have a fear.... I long to grow more godly with each passing day. Call it 'the fear of the Lord,' being in awe of Him and scared to death of any sin that would mar my life."[2]

The other writer is Carole Mayhall, who shares: "Daily I live with [one] fear—a healthy fear if there is such a thing. [It is] that I will miss something God has for me in this life. And it is mind-expanding to contemplate all that He wants me to have. I don't want to be robbed of even one of God's riches by not taking time to let Him invade my life. By not listening to what He is telling me."³

Dear reader, let's join these two women in their "healthy fear" of the life-marring sins that can cause us to miss God's best, that can hinder our desire to walk with Him in all His ways. And if you've already borne the scars of sinful ways, oh, please thank the Lord now for His unspeakable gift of forgiveness and for His marvelous grace to live for Him from this point forward.

*Lesson #3—David went on.*

After the death of his child, "David arose from the ground, washed and anointed himself, and changed his clothes; and he went into the house of the LORD and worshiped...and he ate" (2 Samuel 12:20). A forgiven sinner, the grateful David went on to write many of his most poignant psalms, including the penitential psalms, which expressed his passionate outpouring of confession, a contrite spirit of true repentance, and the sparkling brilliance of joy revived by forgiveness.

And please note—David carried no bitterness toward God. He wholeheartedly accepted the responsibility for his wrongdoings as he wrote, "For I acknowledge my transgressions, and my sin is ever before me. Against You, You only, have I sinned, and done this evil in Your sight—that You may be found just when You speak, and blameless when You judge" (Psalm 51:3,4). David owned his sin and considered the

Lord to be "gracious...and righteous; yes... [and] merciful" (Psalm 116:5).

Beloved, we must follow David's personal example of going on after a season of sin or tragedy. Do you perhaps need to...

get up—rise up from the ground,
wash up—wash yourself,
dress up—change clothes,
look up—enter into the presence of the
Lord,
pray up—spend time in prayer and worship,
eat up—eat a bite,
and then go on?

What marvelous instruction and resolve we draw from dear David! He truly shows us a pattern for spiritual growth. Our role is always to rise up and go on. God's role is to sustain us along the way...and He promises to do just that!

And now, my dear reading friend, let's *lift up* our praise to God, *rise up,* and *go on* our journey with the Lord. Let's taste the 12 promises He offers to us in this brief (only 117 words!) psalm of encouragement and refreshment.

# God's Promise
# of Care

~

*The* L*ORD* *is my shepherd.*
P*SALM* 23:1

*I am the good shepherd;*
*and I know My sheep,*
*and am known by My own.*
J*OHN* 10:14

~

When fear regarding
the cares of this world sets in,
we must remember God's promise
to care for us.
—*Elizabeth George*

$\mathcal{N}$o words ever written have carried the weight or the comfort that these five do—*The LORD is my shepherd.* Youngsters and oldsters alike are soothed and assured by the thought and the promise of God as a personal shepherd to care for them throughout the challenges of life's journey.

I know because I've seen it myself.

When my husband pastored the senior saints at our church, time after time he was asked to read Psalm 23 as someone lay dying and, later, at their memorial service. My own father, up to the time he died at age 96, loved Psalm 23. And then, when Jim and I arrived at my dad's funeral, a tiny bulletin was placed in our hands...and there it was—every word and verse (and promise!) of Psalm 23. Yes, the saint on the deathbed finds solace in the promises of Psalm 23.

And yet the saints alive love it too. At the time I taught this remarkable psalm at the women's Bible study at our church, the hearts of those who listened were touched once again by the thought of the Lord as their own caring shepherd. What kind of women were in our group?

There were women who were being denied the joys of motherhood, whose halls at home were empty for unknown reasons. Women whose nests were filled to overflowing, who were in the throes of the daily busyness of packed, fast-track home life. Women with teens needing so much guidance and yet spurning it. Women whose young adult children were making not-so-wise choices. Women challenged to raise their children alone. Women whose homes were full of grandchildren they were raising. Women facing cancer tests and undergoing surgery and chemotherapy. Women with life-threatening diseases and physical limitations. Women whose husbands were laid off from their jobs. Women who suffered in unhappy marriages, even divorce. Women (like me) who were nursing and losing their parents. Women who were tasting empty nests and bereavement, who were living alone. From every walk and season of life, these were women who loved and needed (oh, so desperately!) the loving care of their Shepherd.

Yes, young and old, well and dying, male and female—*all* love the Twenty-third Psalm, the Shepherd Psalm!

The Shepherd...have you ever wondered how the thought of God as a shepherd originated? In Hebrew, the five English words—*the Lord is my shepherd*—come from two words, *Jehovah-Rohi*. These words translate to "the-LORD-is-my-shepherd."

And what can we learn about our Shepherd, the Lord God, and His promised care from the Bible?

## *Jehovah-Rohi Feeds Us*

One major meaning of the word *shepherd* is "to feed," and here are just a few of its uses:

§ The Bible narrative of Joseph opens with him "*feeding the flock with his brothers*" (Genesis 37:2).

§ Later, in Egypt, when Pharaoh asked Joseph's brothers about their occupation, they answered, "Your servants are shepherds...[and we] have no *pasture* for [our] flocks" (Genesis 47:3-4).

§ Still another glimpse of *rohi* is found when we read that David, the author of Psalm 23, "returned from Saul to *feed* his father's sheep" (1 Samuel 17:15).

§ And finally, in the Shepherd Psalm, we read David's inspired words, "The LORD [Jehovah] is my *shepherd*."

~ ✗ ~

## ~ *Reflecting on God's Promises* ~

Dear one, as one of *Jehovah-Rohi*'s sheep, you have the promise of God to feed you! You and I, as creatures who need physical and spiritual food, enjoy both from the hand of the Shepherd. He cares for us throughout life and brings us to places of pasture. Through circumstances and events, He insures that we are brought to the place where we will feed—and feed on His best.

I'm not a shepherd, but I did work at The Brandeis Institute located in the rolling hills of Simi Valley, California. These lush hills were on the trail of many sheepherders. There at The Institute, the bell at the entrance gate would frequently ring in the spring, as yet another shepherd asked permission to graze his sheep on the property owned by The Institute. A caring and responsible shepherd had led his flock there to feast on the grassy slopes.

This kind of care is the role of a good shepherd—and a role completely fulfilled for us by the Good Shepherd.

And here's another tender fact about a good shepherd—when there are no pastures, he [himself] gathers the food needed for his flock by using his crook to pull down leaves and berries from the trees. Then he feeds his sheep directly and intimately right out of his own hand!

Why should we worry, dear friend?

Why should we worry about food and clothing? About finances and money? About security and the needs of life? We have *Jehovah-Rohi!* We have the Lord as our caring shepherd! When fears regarding the cares of this world set in, we must remember God's promise to care for us. And then we must do as David, the writer of the Shepherd Psalm (and a shepherd himself!), did and declare, "Whenever I am afraid, I will trust in You" (Psalm 56:3)!

*Noise*, too, made my list. The noise of clamoring. The noise of too many people and too much traffic (like ten lanes worth!). The noise of neighbors. The noise of people arguing, of yelling, of anger.

I'm sure you could think of many more situations that would leave us both craving a moment of peace! But good news awaits us right here in verse two: *He leads me beside the still waters.*

> *He*—He, the Shepherd, knows all about our need for peace and provides it. He has made us, He has planned our path, He knows our every challenge, and He provides the peace we need for fulfilling His will for our lives.

> *Leads*—Our Shepherd most definitely leads us to the places where peace is plentiful and makes sure we attain it.

> *Still waters*—He leads us beside still, restful waters of comfort. The last thing you and I need when we're on the edge of collapse is the threatening power of raging waters and thundering rapids. The Shepherd knows this, too. And so He wisely leads us to a peaceful place beside a quiet, tranquil stream.

We can both testify that our souls become dry on a steady diet of stress. We quickly become depleted and weary. We stagger, we stumble, we crumble, and we make errors in judgment...all because we need a time beside the still waters. But, take heart, beloved—*He leads us beside the still waters!*

## ∾ Reflecting on God's Promises ∾

Have you visited the still waters of God's peace and comfort lately?

The waters are there...waiting for you. And the Shepherd is there, too. Refreshment is there. Revival is there. Renewal is there. Comfort is there. And peace is there, too.

God, who gives us His peace, extends rest to the weary and renewal to the exhausted. He wants our souls to be at peace, and He promises to accomplish that peace. Oh, dear friend, drink deeply of Him from His Word! Partake often. Commune with Him in prayer beside His peaceful waters. Allow Him to lead you there now. Make God's still waters "your place."

Oh, the beauty of Psalm 23:2! "He leads me beside the still waters." Here the peace that makes us whole and places us in harmony with God is characterized by cool, fresh water. By the still waters, the rest of peace is enjoyed. As verse two has been translated, "My spirit was lifted and my endurance renewed."

## Meet Jehovah-Shalom, the God of Peace

This seems like a good time to look at another characteristic and name of God that's illustrated in Psalm 23. God's promise in verse two to give us His peace points us to *Jehovah-Shalom*, meaning "Jehovah, my peace" or "Jehovah brings peace." And, just as we've seen with the other names that portray God's character—*Jehovah-Rohi* and *Jehovah-Jireh*—this name is derived from God's dealings with His people.

We first meet *Jehovah-Shalom* in the book of Judges when the reigning judge, Gideon, "built an altar...to the LORD, and called it The-LORD-Shalom," which means "Jehovah is peace" (6:24). God's people were involved in a repeated cycle of sin at this time in their history. Things got worse and worse as...

God's people had begun to forget Jehovah, their God.
    Instead, they were turning to the gods of the people
    around them.
        Truly it was a time when everyone did what
        was right in his own eyes (Judges 21:25)!
            Finally God's people corrupted
            themselves with idolatries and
            abominations.
                As a result, they lost their
                purity, prosperity, freedom,
                and peace.

Down, down, down went God's chosen people, the apple of His eye! Soon a desperate pattern of sin-punishment-repentance-deliverance emerged. It was a dark, dark, dark time for the Israelites, a time of alternating prosperity and adversity, of repenting and sinning, of deliverance and slavery. There was definitely no peace in their roller-coaster existence!

## *Meet Gideon, the Judge*

Enter Gideon, the fifth judge appointed by God to lead and deliver His people.

We first meet Gideon in his own dark place, hiding in a winepress for fear of the Midianites, the enemies of the Israelites. Gideon had scraped together a scant handful of wheat that the enemy hadn't destroyed and was secretly threshing it (Judges 6:11).

Into this dark scene in this dark time in the history of the children of God, the Angel of Jehovah suddenly, brilliantly, and wondrously appeared to Gideon! The angel promised deliverance for God's people and called Gideon to lead them.

Poor Gideon! He doubted. He hesitated. He questioned. He wondered. He squirmed. He feared.

But the Lord led Gideon to the still waters and stilled his fears with these comforting words: "Peace be with you; do not fear, you shall not die" (6:23).

Then Gideon worshiped. (Wouldn't you?!) He built an altar to the Lord and named it *Jehovah-Shalom,* meaning "The Altar of Peace with Jehovah" (6:24). This wonderful label signified Gideon's confident anticipation of God's promise of not only victory, but also long-awaited and much-needed peace.

∾ ❧ ∾

## ∾ *Reflecting on God's Promises* ∾

I certainly don't want us to dwell on any negatives, but we can learn a lesson from the Israelites here. The lack of peace that they experienced clearly shows us the importance of obedience in our quest to know God's peace. Our "reflections on God's promises" have been opportunities for us to stop and think, and I feel like we need to do just that right now.

Is your daily life characterized by trouble, chaos, and disaster? Do you feel like you're living under the pile, always behind, making little or no progress, that things are always out of control or never quite in order? In short, does your life lack the mark of God's peace on it? Is there an absence of *Jehovah-Shalom*?

Of course, events and crises will disrupt the peaceful pattern of life. But it's also true that we know in our heart of hearts when things are not right between us and the Lord. We know when our wandering ways are resulting in turmoil. Yes, we definitely know when we are failing in our love and obedience to Jehovah!

Why not give some thought to your walk with God? As our verse here guarantees, *He leads*. But we, dear one, must heed. He leads, but we must follow.

And then reflect on these thoughts.

❧  *Loving the* LORD *is not an emotional goosebump; it is a commitment to selfless obedience.*          —John MacArthur

❧  *Our part is to trust God fully, to obey Him implicitly, and to follow His instructions faithfully.*          —V. Raymond Edman

§ *To know God is to experience His love in Christ, and to return that love in obedience.* —C. H. Dodd

~ ~ ~ ~ ~ ~ ~ ᴥ ~ ~ ~ ~ ~ ~

~ ᴥ ~

## ~ *Reflecting Again on God's Promises* ~

But there's another kind of following that has nothing to do with disobedience and everything to do with commitment. This was Gideon's situation. Fear and doubt caused him to hesitate in his commitment to the Lord. And the result was a definite lack of peace in his life.

And, my friend, fear and doubt affect women just like you and me, too. Let me explain...

One year I met a lady in the Pacific Northwest who was struggling with commitment. On a break during my seminar, this dear woman poured out her problem to me. No, there was no blatant sin in her life. There were no glaring areas of disobedience. There was no stubborn refusal to follow the Lord. There was simply a personal and serious life-challenge. And her refusal to take the challenge was causing this lady obvious turmoil!

The challenge was born the day this precious sister in Christ went with her husband to a missions conference. It was a thrilling time for both of them. But at the end of the conference, each person was given a simple three-by-five-inch card with only these words on it:

```
Any thing
Any where
Any time
At any cost


_____        _____
(date)                 (signature)
```

The speaker at the gathering was simply asking each person to prayerfully sign and date the card with the four **A**'s.

"Honey, can I borrow your pen?" my friend's husband whispered immediately. As she handed him her pen, she noticed that he could hardly wait to sign away! It was no problem for *him*!

Oh, but in *her* heart the struggle had begun. *Any thing? Any where? Any time? At any cost?* No, she just couldn't sign. She had to pray. Truly, the challenge pierced deeply...to her very soul...and her spirit was in an upheaval!

But my story doesn't end here...and neither does my friend's. Nearly five years later, at another women's conference in Washington, guess who walked up to me during the break? This friend who had struggled so! But this time she was able to finish her story. She literally glowed as she shared that, after seven months— *seven months!*—of prayer and agonizing and fitful heart-searching, she had finally signed her card. In fact, it was a treasure that she carried in her Bible and pulled out to show to me.

And now for you, dear one. Could you join with this dear saint (and her husband!) in following God's Leading? Could you sign the four A's? Could you sing along with the hymnwriter, "Where He leads me, I will follow—I'll go with Him, with Him all the way"?[2] (And, we might add, *any where, any time,* and *at any cost!*)

God's role is to lead us. But ours, beloved, is to follow.

So...how are you doing in the following department? Have you looked full into the Shepherd's wonderful face and into His eyes of love and whispered, "Truly, dear Lord, where You lead me, I will follow"? Do these words express the deep sentiment of your heart? And, more importantly, are you following Him? If so, then you are truly enjoying God's promise of peace. ∼ ∼ ∼ ∼ ∼ ❧ ∼ ∼ ∼ ∼ ∼

## Meet Gideon, the Warrior

But I want us to also hear the end of Gideon's story. As you remember, when we met him he was cowering in a hole trying to thresh out some grain for food without being seen by his enemies (Judges 6:11). That's when the Angel of the Lord appeared...

with a proclamation—"...you shall save Israel from the hand of the Midianites" (verse 14),

with a promise—"Surely I will be with you, and you shall defeat the Midianites..." (verse 16),

with peace—"Peace be with you; do not fear..." (verse 23), and

with power—"The LORD is with you, you mighty man of valor!" (verse 12).

And the result? These assurances and gifts from God transformed Gideon from being fearful to being a fearless leader of God's people. As the fifth judge, Gideon acted with confidence, defeated the Midianite army, excelled as a military strategist, was offered the title of king, and was inducted into God's "Hall of Faith" in Hebrews 11.

∾ ☙ ∾

### ∾ *Reflecting on God's Promises* ∾

Do you remember Gideon's initial responses to God's call to service? They included doubt... hesitation...questioning...wondering...squirming... and fear. These are certainly not responses that suggest peace of mind! But, unfortunately, they are responses that sometimes define you and me as we go through life.

Do any of these words currently describe you in your walk with God? Is He attempting to lead the hesitant, reticent sheep in you? Is He trying to use you in mighty ways for His purposes...while you hem and haw, dawdle and fidget, fuss and fume, and stew and worry?

We fail to have peace, dear one, when we forget (like Gideon did) that God never asks for *us* to have confidence. He only asks that we have confidence in *Him!* When God commands, God supplies.

And what did God supply to Gideon so that He could valiantly fulfill God's command? He promised Gideon that He would give him the strength He needed. Gideon was a simple farmer, but when enabled and strengthened by God, the simple farmer was transformed into a mighty warrior, a mighty man of valor (verse 12), a man of mighty faith (Hebrews 11:32)!

The same transformation is possible for us, too, my friend. Our obedience—a true mark of our faith—allows God to transform the meek into the mighty! God will do the transforming— that's His role. But we must do the yielding— that's our role.

So...are you trusting in the Lord? And are you allowing Him who is mighty to do great things in...and through...and for...you? God promises you'll not only know His peace as you look to His promises, but you'll also know His power!

## *Meet the Prince of Peace*

Before we finish verse two and our visit to the still waters, we need to behold the Prince of Peace. To enjoy peace and harmony with God means to enjoy the harmony of a relationship with God. And it is Jesus Christ, the Prince of Peace (Isaiah 9:6), who makes a relationship with God possible. Peace with God includes...

- *harmony*—to be in harmony with God due to the payment of a debt.

- *a peace offering*—restored fellowship between God and man, accomplished only by shed blood (see the peace offering of Leviticus 3).

Dear one, Jesus, the Prince of Peace, satisfies both of these definitions of peace.

∾ ✣ ∾

## ∾ *Reflecting on God's Promises* ∾

And now it's time for the most important "reflection" you'll spend in this book. It's time to make sure that you truly belong to Christ, that you are truly in the family of God, that you're a Christian who enjoys the peace of God and the God of peace.

So I must ask you: Are you a child of God? Have you been reconciled to God through His Son, Jesus Christ? Are your sins washed white as snow by the shed blood of Jesus? Is He your Savior, your Shepherd of Peace?

Just to be sure the path to God is absolutely clear to you, prayerfully consider these facts:

§ The fact of sin—Romans 3:23 states, "All have sinned and fall short of the glory of God."

§ The fact of judgment—Romans 6:23 teaches us that "the wages of sin is death, but the gift of God is eternal life in Christ Jesus our Lord."

§ The fact of Christ's death for sins— Romans 5:8 tells us that "God demonstrates His own love toward us, in that while we were still sinners, Christ died for us."

§ The fact of acceptance of Christ by faith—Romans 10:9 shows us the way: "If you confess with your mouth the Lord Jesus and believe in your heart that God has raised Him from the dead, you will be saved."

§ The fact of peace—Romans 5:1 tells us that "having been justified by faith, we have peace with God through our Lord Jesus Christ."

If you're not yet God's child, make this time of "reflection" your time of accepting Christ by faith. Your peace will begin immediately!

And if you're already a child of God, spend your time of "reflection" thanking and praising Him for the peace He extends to you through His Son, Jesus Christ.

## —*A Prayer for Peace*—

And now, dear Lord, we acknowledge afresh that
You are the God of all peace, *Jehovah-Shalom.*
You offer us Your peace. Ours is to receive.
You give us Your peace. Ours is to take.
You lead us to Your still waters. Ours is to follow.
You extend Your hand. Ours is to take hold.
May we enjoy Your presence and
the tranquility of the still waters
where You pour out your promise of peace.
Amen.

# ~5~

# *God's Promise of Healing*

~

*He restores my soul.*
PSALM 23:3

*Praise the LORD!…*
*He heals the brokenhearted*
*and binds up their wounds.*
PSALM 147:1,3

~

Our wonderful Shepherd
not only takes care of our physical requirements:
He also sees to our spiritual needs.
He ministers to the spirit and soul
as well as the physical body.
—*Elizabeth George*

*B*ecause Jim and I are active in ministry, it seems like we know more than our share of widows. We've been through the season of widowhood with Jim's dear mother—twice! And we've walked through the valley of the shadow of death with many of the dear ladies in the seniors' class Jim once pastored...emerging with them on the other side when they stepped out of that dark valley without a partner. Some of the women's losses were tragic, announced simply and finally by a ring of the telephone and a voice bearing the awful news of their loss. Others suffered daily as they watched their beloved husbands linger on through cancer or decline. Both extremes—and everything in between—are hard to handle.

We know that death for any of God's children is an ultimate victory and precious in His sight (Psalm 116:15!). But still, the loss of a loved one is painful for the one left behind, for the one who must go on walking with the Shepherd alone, pressed into yet another new season of life.

And certainly, there are other hardships in life that are devastating. Disability. The physical suffering of surgery, cancer, illness, an accident. The collapse of the family. Rejection. Disappointment. Betrayal. Calamity. The list goes on.

And so must life.

But our question is...*How? How* are we to go on? *How* are we to cope with these sapping certainties of life? And *what* are you and I to do to handle life after a life-altering incident?

This, dear one, is where God once again comes to our rescue. In our times of pain and sorrow, God's tender care goes into action with His promise to heal us. As the psalmist's four words so beautifully state, "He restores my soul" (Psalm 23:3).

Looking back for a moment at what we've learned about what it means to be one of the Great Shepherd's sheep, our conclusions are staggering!

—We have the promise of His care and provision (verse 1).
—We have the promise of His rest and peace (verse 2).

And now we taste yet another promise—that of the Lord's healing restoration (verse 3). Our wonderful Shepherd not only takes care of our physical requirements—He also sees to our spiritual needs. He ministers to the spirit and soul as well as the physical body. God's abundant provision revives us physically, but in this present promise—*He restores my soul*—we witness the Lord healing us spiritually.

## The Character of Jehovah-Rophe

There's another name of God that I think fits here as we're discussing the promise of God's healing restoration—the name *Jehovah-Rophe* (pronounced ró-fáy). This wondrous name means "the LORD heals," and there's a remarkable history behind it. Here's what happened...

After God's people were released from their bondage in Egypt and delivered from Pharaoh's army at the Red Sea, they journeyed into new territory. Jubilant and still marveling over God's many miracles on their behalf, the Israelites stepped into their dream future...only to find there was no water to drink. Moving on, water was finally discovered at Marah...but it was bitter and undrinkable (Exodus 15).

Then Moses, who had been a shepherd himself for 40 years, remembered the One who takes care of His sheep and cried out for help to the Lord...and He answered. Jehovah then showed Moses a tree, which, when cast into the bitter water, instantly made it sweet. Jehovah provided, announcing, "For I am the LORD who heals you" (Exodus 15:26).

What an object lesson this encounter with *Jehovah-Rophe*, the Lord who heals, must have been for the Israelites (and for us)! God's people were dying of thirst with only bitter, poisonous water on hand. And God took their physical need and turned it into a spiritual issue. Out of a bitter experience God revealed Himself in yet another sweet, comforting way, as "Jehovah heals."

## *The Cast-Down Sheep*

In the Old Testament, "to heal" is often used of a physician and means *to restore* or *to cure*. And just who does *Jehovah-Rophe*, the Great Physician, heal? He heals and restores those of His who are cast down.

There's a beautiful picture for us here. You see, shepherds throughout time have applied the term "cast-down" to any sheep that's turned over on its back and can't get up again by itself. The scene goes something like this...

A heavy, fat, or long-fleeced sheep will lie down comfortably in a little hollow in the ground. Next it rolls over on its side to stretch out and relax in the green grasses. But suddenly the center of gravity in its body shifts, pitching the sheep onto its back so that its feet no longer touch the ground! Despite the poor sheep's struggling efforts, it becomes impossible for it to turn upright.

This is a sheep that is "cast down." And, interestingly, it's usually the largest and strongest sheep that are the most easily cast down! If it's cool or cloudy or rainy, a cast-down sheep can survive in this position for a day or two. But if the weather is hot and sunny, a cast-down sheep will be in critical condition in just a few hours! It's vital that the shepherd arrive on the scene soon or the sheep will die.

## The Course of Restoration

As I read about the process of restoration as described by a shepherd in New Zealand, there seemed to be three stages involved.

*Stage 1—Finding the cast-down sheep.* The caring, compassionate shepherd knows each and every one of his sheep. And he also knows when one of his flock is missing and sets out to find his wayward sheep, searching and surveying the range for the obvious form of a sheep in an unnatural position.

*Stage 2—Restoring the cast-down sheep.* Restoration can be quite involved, depending on the condition of the cast-down sheep. If, for instance, the sheep has been in its helpless condition for only a short time, all it takes from the shepherd is a gentle roll of the sheep over onto its feet, and, with only a few stumbles and wobbles, that fortunate sheep is back on its way to the fold.

However, if the poor sheep has been cast down for some time, restoring it takes a great deal of patience, time, and care. First the sheep is gently rolled over. Then its legs are rubbed and massaged by the shepherd to revive circulation. Next comes the miserable sheep's head, which is propped up on the shepherd's knee and stroked and caressed and held for a time by its loving caregiver. Following this tender attention, the sheep is physically lifted up onto its feet by the shepherd. As the weak and wobbly sheep leans against the strong legs of its shepherd, the sheep takes its first few steps, fully supported by its master. It may take a full hour to get the sheep walking again, until finally it can stagger away on its own legs circling near the shepherd, who may have to rush over and pick his sheep up again...and again...and again.

*Stage 3—Following the cast-down sheep.* But the shepherd isn't done yet! For not until the sheep that's been cast down takes its first bites of green grass does the shepherd know that all is well. And so the good shepherd follows and checks up on his repairing sheep...until it is fully restored.[1]

## ∽ *Reflecting on God's Promises* ∽

And now it's time to shift from sheep to the soul.

Life is hard! We're both familiar with its hurts and pains and inconveniences. You and I have tasted life's trials and sorrows. Unfortunately, many women are broken in spirit and crushed in heart and soul. Indeed, the prospects of becoming cast down are high as each new dawn and every new corner looms fully loaded with trouble.

I don't mean to sound negative. No, I'm just stating the facts of life—coping is a life-long challenge. But the good news is that we have a shepherd—the Good Shepherd—to walk with us along life's way. We have...

§ *Jehovah-Rohi* who promises to care for us,

§ *Jehovah-Jireh* who promises to provide for us,

§ *Jehovah-Shalom* who promises to give us peace, and

§ *Jehovah-Rophe* who promises to restore us.

So, as New Zealand shepherd W. G. Bowen points out, "Problems are not the problem, but the problem is in trying to cope with problems on our own and with our own resources and in our own strength, or weakness, without the help of the Shepherd."[2]

Armed with the promise of healing restoration and confident in the presence of the Shepherd, you and I, dear one, can walk through all of life. With the help of the Lord, we can handle its challenges and heartaches, even the valley of the shadow of death. What comfort it should bring to our fainting hearts to know that in those stumbling times of discouragement and

despair, of depletion and seeming defeat, the
Shepherd will find us...restore and "fix" us...and
follow us...until we are well on our way again!

~ ~ ~ ~ ~ ✤ ~ ~ ~ ~ ~

# The Case of Elijah, the Cast-Down Sheep

Are you wondering what causes us to need God's healing
touch? What is it that takes us down or tempts us to give up?
One such cause of demise is *not enough of the right things* (or,
put another way, *too much of the wrong things!*). For instance,
when we've been...

> running too long—the Shepherd must revive us.
> running on empty—the Shepherd must refresh us.
> running with the wrong people—the Shepherd
> must replace them.
> running away—the Shepherd must retrieve us.
> running scared—the Shepherd must refocus us.

Do you remember my earlier statement that it's generally
the largest and strongest sheep that become cast down? Well,
in the Bible that certainly proved true. We see Elijah, the most
famous and dramatic of Israel's prophets, a man who performed many miracles for God (and one of God's largest and
strongest sheep!), succumbing to the problem of not enough
of the right things.

Elijah was God's representative in a showdown with the
priests of Baal and Asherah (1 Kings 18). After calling down
fire from heaven and after overseeing the slaughter of all 450

of the false prophets of Baal, something happened—Elijah received word that Ahab's wife Jezebel was seeking to kill him (1 Kings 19). *One woman* was after him!

And so this great man of faith ran for his life, running and running...

...and he ran away into the wilderness

...and he ran too long

...and he ran too hard

...and he ran scared

and he ran so far and so long and so hard that soon he was running on empty.

Falling down in weariness (much like a cast-down sheep!) Elijah rolled over and stuck his worn-out feet into the air and gave up. He even asked God to let him die—indeed, to kill him! And then the largest and strongest of God's prophets passed out in an exhausted sleep.

How did God bring healing to His servant Elijah and restore him to usefulness?

He gave him physical care—rest, food, and drink.

He talked with him and listened to his discouragement, to his dismay, to his feelings of futility.

He gave him something to do.

He gave him a plan and some facts (1 Kings 19:4-18).

God kept right on in His ministry of restoring His precious prophet, never letting go and never giving up on him.

~ ❧ ~

## ~ Reflecting on God's Promises ~

Oh dear! If the largest and the strongest sheep succumb to exhaustion, discouragement, and depression, is there any hope for little ewes like you and me?

But, dear one, before you and I give up, we must realize that the causes *and* the cures are the same for us as they were for Elijah, one of the largest sheep of all!

We noted that God gave Elijah something to do. Why? Because, you see, Elijah had gotten *too comfortable*. He perhaps even liked moping around, sleeping, lying on the ground in a heap! And he'd gotten *too fat*. He certainly hadn't done much in over 40 days! And he'd gotten *too independent*—he had left his servant and assistant and companion behind and gone on alone. Yes, we would agree that Elijah needed something to do...and that was a part of God's cure.

Do you perhaps fit "the Elijah profile"? Are you depressed or dismayed? Defeated or discouraged? Are you alone? Are you tired of it all—and from it all? Then check out your situation.

§ Have you gotten *too comfortable*? Are you lying around too much? Nibbling and nodding a little too often? Sprawled out in the green grass a little longer than necessary? Then do something!

§ Have you gotten *too fat?* When was the last time you really stretched yourself in some worthy effort? Really dug in and gave something your all? Really paid a price for something meaningful? Then do something!

§ Have you gotten *too independent?* The Bible tells us that being with others in the church body stimulates us, inciting us to good deeds and noble actions (Hebrews 10:24). God's people bring joy into our lives, keep us company, keep us on the right track, and keep us out of trouble! So do something!

Beloved, something to do is one of God's cures for the cast down—so let's take the cure! Let's do something!

~ ~ ~ ~ ~ ❧ ~ ~ ~ ~ ~

## ~ *Reflecting Again on God's Promises* ~

The Lord heals. It's so like our Lord to pursue us, to continue after us when we run, to supply all our needs when we choose not enough of the right things and too much of the wrong things! But is there a prescription for us that will help us to stand upright instead of becoming cast down?

Try these two surefire remedies for health and healing.

*Feed on God's Word.* Beloved, *He*, the Shepherd, restores our soul—not TV, not entertainment, not a sit-com, not food, not a drink, not a drug, not a vacation, and not another trip to the mall. And one way to touch the Shepherd and to experience the promise of His healing touch is to touch His Word. We know that "the law of the LORD is perfect, restoring the soul" (Psalm 19:7 NASB), and we can have direct contact with the Lord by feeding on His Word.

*Commune with the Shepherd in prayer.* Read another lesson on "shepherd-ology" from our friend from New Zealand:

It is interesting to note that [in a flock] each sheep has a time of quietness and aloneness with his shepherd every day. Early in the morning the sheep would form a grazing line and keep the same position throughout the day. At some time along the way each sheep left the grazing line and went to the shepherd. The shepherd received the sheep with outstretched arms speaking kindly to it. The sheep would rub against the shepherd's leg, or if the shepherd were seated, rub its cheek against his face. Meanwhile the shepherd would gently pat the sheep, rubbing its nose and ears and

> scratching its chin. After a brief period of this intimate fellowship together, the sheep returned to its place in the grazing line.[3]
>
> What a blessing to be able to leave the cares of life for a brief period and spend time in the outstretched arms of the Shepherd, rubbing, as it were, our cheek against His face in intimate fellowship through prayer!

Well, my friend, our sweet time here in verse three is almost over. Do you yet have your answer to the question we posed at the beginning of this chapter? About *how* can we possibly go on when life has knocked us down? Cast us down?

I hope you now know that you can always go on because of the Shepherd and His healing touch. He comes after you in your pain and your utter despair, when you are down—so far down that you can no longer get up. And He touches you.

He heals your spirit.

He restores you when you're cast down.

He retrieves and fetches you home again when you wander.

He draws you back when you're unsure.

He relieves you when you're hurt.

He rescues you when you're in danger.

And He finds you when you're lost.

Oh, give praise to and for the Shepherd now, for He restores your soul! The Good Shepherd finds and heals His sheep! Or, as verse three is also translated, "He found me when I was cast down and gave life to me again."[4]

That's what your wonderful Shepherd does for you and me, dear one. No matter what happens in life, no matter how or how often you become cast down, God "heals" you. He restores you. He gives you life again...to go on with Him.

# ~6~

# *God's Promise*
# *of Guidance*

~

*He leads me in the paths of righteousness*
*for His name's sake.*
PSALM 23:3

*I will instruct you and teach you*
*in the way you should go;*
*I will guide you with My eye.*
PSALM 32:8

~

Just as you notice the *ways* of your household,
so God notices the *ways* of your paths.
Just as you hurt and agonize over those you love,
so He cares for you.
And just as you move to guide your flock back
onto a more profitable path,
so God guides you "in the paths of righteousness."
—*Elizabeth George*

$\mathcal{I}$t takes 21 days to eliminate a bad habit and replace it with a new one." Are you familiar with this simplistic law of behavior change? Better yet, have you tried it?

I know I have...numerous times—and with numerous habits! From seeking to develop the habit of prayer, to stopping in-between-meal snacking, to better use of time—I've tried this "21-day miracle cure." But I've found that it takes much longer to break old habits and create new ones. It just seems that the old ways (which for me are many times the "bad" ways, or the "wrong" ways, or the "lesser" ways!) are so deeply ingrained that it almost seems impossible to improve or change them.

And that's because of *repetition*. A habit (according to Mr. Webster's dictionary) is a custom or practice acquired by *repetition*. A habit is an action that, due to *repetition*, increases in performance and decreases in resistance. Thus, by *repetition* an action becomes automatic, and a habit—good or bad—is born.

But, my friend, there's hope for our habits! Psalm 23, verse three, reveals yet another role the Shepherd takes in our lives—*He leads [us] in the paths of righteousness for His name's sake.* If we stay close beside Him and walk where He guides us, our habits will honor His name, and we'll harvest the fruits of righteousness. We'll develop holy habits!

So let's step out onto the Shepherd's path and learn what it means to have His promise to guide us and what it means to walk in His ways. First, the "paths"...

## *The "Paths"*

A very simple way to understand the "paths" of righteousness into which the Good Shepherd leads you and me is by the word "tracks." In bygone days, tracks were made by the frequent passage of wagons. The more often a path was taken, the deeper the tracks cut into the soil, until they became plain and obvious. Eventually deep ruts developed.

When I was studying in Israel in preparation for writing my book *Beautiful in God's Eyes: The Treasures of the Proverbs 31 Woman,* I saw the same thing happen regarding the "paths" sheep take on the hillsides. Because sheep habitually take the same way each time they go out to graze, their paths cut deep patterns into the sides of the slopes. In fact, many of the mountains look terraced—just because the sheep paths have worn the soil into stair-step ledges.

Then, later, as I was actually writing my book on the life of the Proverbs 31 woman (Proverbs 31:10-31), I discovered there in the Bible passage (in verse 27) the use of "paths" or "ways" or "tracks"—"she watches over the *ways* of her household." These words picture a woman acting as a shepherdess to her household. She carefully notices the patterns of her home life. These are the *ways* of her household, the general comings and goings, the habits and activities of the people at home. The Hebrew word for *ways* means literal tracks made by constant use. They're like the footpath that cuts across a lawn due to repeated use.

Well, the beautiful overseer-of-the-home from Proverbs 31 observes all that goes on in her home. Our watchwoman is aware of all habits and any changes in habits. Nothing catches her by surprise. She keeps up to the minute on the status of her family members and the general flow of her home. She's aware of everything that goes on within its walls.[1]

## ∞ *Reflecting on God's Promises* ∞

Let's stop a moment and consider your own heart and home. If you have a family, think about how deeply you love and care for that family. About how concerned you are about the pattern of each precious life under your roof. Every mother and homemaker knows the pain of watching one of her flock struggle, stumble, and stray. We hurt as those we love make choices that lead them down unhealthy paths. We dread the sure and awful outcomes that await our loved ones if they continue down such dreadful paths.

Yes, we hurt...but we also act! With hearts wrung with agony, we roll up our mothering sleeves and do all we can to correct the situation. We create new rules and set narrower boundaries. We institute new disciplinary methods that carry more severe consequences.

And why? All because of love—parental love.

Now, can you begin to grasp the Shepherd's great divine love for His sheep? Just as you notice the *ways* of your household, so God notices the *ways* of your paths. Just as you hurt and agonize over those you love, so He cares for you. And just as you move to correct and guide your flock back onto a more profitable path, so God leads and guides you in "the paths of righteousness."

~ ~ ~ ~ ~ ❧ ~ ~ ~ ~ ~

## *The Paths of "Righteousness"*

So far, we know that our Shepherd is leading us. And He's leading us in "paths." And now we discover that those paths are paths of "righteousness." That means they're stiff or straight paths. For instance, in the Bible *righteousness* is used in these ways:

§ *With men,* righteousness indicated a full measure. Measurements and weights were to be just and right.

§ *With God,* righteousness indicated a full measure in the spiritual sense—offering to Him what was sincere versus half-hearted and shoddy.

§ *With a court,* righteousness indicated a full measure of righteous judgment. Judges and officers were to render justice and make things right.

Stiff and straight. This doesn't sound very pretty or seem too desirable in our loose times, does it? But, dear one, we have a God who is zealously interested in righteousness, and we have a God who promises to guide us into righteous paths.

∾ ❧ ∾

## ∾ *Reflecting on God's Promises* ∾

It's true that we live in an age that honors looseness. Praise abounds for those who can "flex and flow," who can roll with the tide, who can give and take, who are skilled at compromise and in finding the middle ground.

But we're the righteous saints of a righteous God! And He makes sure we walk in His stiff, straight paths of righteousness! And He is faithful to tell us in His Word exactly what those paths are. He clearly spells out what He considers to be right and wrong...what He's determined is in and out...what He brands as good and evil. Gracious in other areas, God is stiff and straight about *His* way! In fact, He labels *His* way as *the* way and commands that we walk in it—"This is *the* way, walk in it" (Isaiah 30:21, emphasis added)! As the Shepherd whose responsibility it is to guide us, He plainly defines "the paths of righteousness" and guides us there.

∾ ∾ ∾ ∾ ❧ ∾ ∾ ∾ ∾

## The God of Righteousness

Considering this concept of God's righteousness makes this a good time to introduce yet another wonderful name of our wonderful Lord, *Jehovah-Tsidkenu* (pronounced sid-káy'noo). This name of God means "Jehovah our righteousness" and first appears in Jeremiah 23:5-6. Here are a few brief facts about the scene.

— The kingdom of Judah was falling apart.

— Judah was sinning grievously, even polluting the house of the Lord.

— God sent His prophets to warn His erring people, but their messages went unheeded.

— God, therefore, sent His prophet Jeremiah to predict that Judah would be taken captive.

That was the bad news!

But, because of God's promise to King David to establish his kingdom forever (2 Samuel 7:16), Jeremiah also prophesied some good news—Israel would be restored to the land, and Jehovah would raise up to David a Righteous Branch—*Jehovah Tsidkenu* (Jeremiah 23:5-6).

In short, God was dealing with His sinning people, and they would be chastised. But in the end, God would restore them, and He would produce a Righteous Branch (*Jehovah-Tsidkenu*). That Righteous Branch of David we now know was the Messiah, Jesus Christ.

## ∿ Reflecting on God's Promises ∿

It only seems wise for us to pause and consider the example (albeit a negative one!) of God's people right here before us. They had strayed from God's ways, sinned grievously, and failed to pay attention to God's pleas and instructions. Therefore, they were chastised.

And so, as women who love the Lord, we must bluntly ask ourselves if there is any area in our life where we know we are off track, out of God's will, and have wandered off His path of righteousness. Is there any choice of disobedience we are making repeatedly that is becoming an unholy habit?

I can think of several time-proven practices that will help us to leave the rut of our bad habits and the bypaths of sin and rush to the side (and safety!) of God's guidance:

Admit your sin—and acknowledge it as disobedience.

Ask for accountability—from other trusted Christians.

Arm yourself adequately—with prayer and with Scripture.

Associate with other Christians—who possess the habits you desire.

**A**bolish all stumbling-stones—from your environment.

**A**im at walking beside the Shepherd—one day at a time.

**A**cquaint yourself more intimately with Jesus—and His righteousness.

How blessed we are to have a God who cares for us, who promises to lead us and guide us out of our own unprofitable ruts and into His paths of righteousness!

~ ~ ~ ~ ~ ❧ ~ ~ ~ ~ ~

## *The Purpose of God's Guidance*

But, besides His great love for us, there's a greater reason for God's guidance in our lives—He leads us in the paths of righteousness *for His name's sake,* to bring glory to Himself! You see, in Hebrew thought, a name was normally connected to the character and personality of the bearer's name, and this beautiful phrase—"for His name's sake"—means maintaining one's reputation. God's name points not only to a title for Him, but to His very nature.

Therefore, for *His* sake He leads us to do what is right. Why? Because if *we*, His sheep, sin and stray, we tarnish *His* reputation! So, for the sake of His own name, as well as for our good, He points us in the right direction.[2] His name is *Shepherd* (Psalm 23:1), and if He fails to care for and lead His sheep, He fails to be a Shepherd. Therefore, He must shepherd and care for us because His name demands it.

# ❧ *Reflecting on God's Promises* ❧

And now I want us to go back again to parenting as a picture of God's care and guidance, if you will. I remember all too well when Jim and I were up to our elbows in the business of childraising. Peer pressure on our girls was beginning to create some serious challenges for our family. It was at that time that Jim, as the shepherd of our household, began reminding our daughters that they were a part of "the George household" and that in "the George household" our standards were such-and-such. Many times he told our girls, "We don't do that in the George household," or "That behavior's okay for others...but not for the Georges."

You see, far from being legalistic or demanding, Jim was setting a standard for our family and leading us as a family under the banner of that standard...for his (in this case Jim's) sake. *Jim's* reputation as head-of-household was at stake! *Jim's* character was on trial through the conduct of his family (1 Timothy 3:4). Why? Because, as our head, Jim was responsible and accountable to God for loving and leading us in the right direction—God's direction.

And don't you think we all benefited from having standards set for us by a loving and concerned leader? Many a "wrong" decision and

"wrong" choice and "wrong" path was diverted
because of loving leadership. And it's not that
less-than-perfect decisions weren't made, nor
that "Shepherd Jim" didn't have to go out into
a few highways and byways and fetch his sheep in
from time to time (because, after all, sheep do
have minds of their own!). But the general pattern in our household was loving leadership and
faithful following.

And now, dear one, can you relate this
simple, daily, familiar illustration of family life to
your own faithful following of the Shepherd? He
is faithfully guiding and lovingly leading. And
He has set forth His standards, His path, in His
Word. And His name and reputation are at stake.

So...is your following bringing glory to His
name? He is leading you in the paths of righteousness *for His name's sake*. Are you following
in those paths *for His name's sake?*

## ∾ *Reflecting Again on God's Promises* ∾

And exactly how does God guide you and
me in the paths of His righteousness? These two
practices have never failed to show me God's
path:

*#1—Bible reading.* As someone has well
warned, "Make sure the path you choose leads
you at last to a place where you want to be. A

careful traveler will study the road map before setting out!" Beloved, our road map for the right path is the Bible. Between the covers of our Bible we have the mind—and the map—of God! Indeed, His Word is a lamp unto our feet, ever lighting the path of righteousness...one step and one decision at a time (Psalm 119:105)!

*#2—Prayer.* When we were missionaries in Singapore, I learned from an artist who attended my Bible study that in traditional Chinese painting, there is just one outstanding object, usually a flower. That one flower on the canvas of our life, dear one, is the will of God. God promises to guide us into His paths when we sincerely seek His will. When we chart out the road map with earnest prayer, we'll end up on His path—the right path!

Dear one, God is fulfilling His promise to guide you. Enjoying the blessings that come with this promise will depend on how closely you follow. As a final heart-check, pray over these questions. Your answers will indicate how well you are following.

What are the desires of my heart? Is my first desire to be in God's will—no matter what it is and no matter what it costs?

Am I living my life in a way that honors the Lord, that exhibits to the whole watching world what the paths of righteousness are?

Am I walking near the Shepherd—as close as I can— delighting in His guidance and allowing nothing to distract me from His paths?

And am I willing to go where He guides me...in the paths of righteousness...for His name's sake?

# ~7~

# God's Promise of Presence

~

*Yea, though I walk through*
*the valley of the shadow of death,*
*I will fear no evil; for You are with me.*
PSALM 23:4

*...Lo, I am with you always,*
*even to the end of the age.*
MATTHEW 28:20

~

Just as we must go out into the dark night
to behold the brilliance of the stars,
so God's presence shines brightest
in our valleys of deep darkness.
—*Elizabeth George*

*T*he area where I live in Southern California is considered desert, but, believe it or not, we do receive enough rainfall each year to keep things alive! However, I do remember one seven-year stretch when our area was assessed as emergency drought status. Water use was restricted. Public ads on TV educated us on conservation. No longer could we hose off our driveways and patios. Nor could we wash our cars using a hose. And our lawns could only be watered on certain odd-even days at specific hours of the day and for an assigned number of minutes.

In the beginning of these drought years, one of my friends moved to a new home in the local mountains. Observing the fire codes, she planted vegetation to keep her hillside from eroding and installed the prescribed automatic watering system to keep her foliage alive and protect her home against fire. And each time I visited her, I could see some growth in her landscaping.

But on one of my visits, I remarked about the suddenly glorious hillside vegetation, obvious in the flaming flowers and lushness of maturity. I've never forgotten my hostess's comment: "It's because of the rain. All sunshine produces a desert...but rain brings forth flowers."

Yes! That was it! I hadn't thought about it, but our drought was over! (In fact, we'd been inundated with rain...bringing with it other problems—mud slides and flash floods!) We'd been through seven years of sunshine, but the *rain* had brought this abundance of growth! The *storms* had incited her plants to swell and surge. The darkness of *clouds* had brought about brilliance. What my friend said was true: All sunshine produces a desert...but rain brings forth flowers.

And, dear reader, so it is with life. As we walk through life beside our faithful Shepherd, the path of righteousness stretches not only through the sunshiny green pastures and beside glistening still waters...but also winds down through the dark valley of the shadow of death.

## The Way of the Path

As we continue our walk through Psalm 23, suddenly the path turns downward here in verse 4. It begins to wind around unannounced corners. There's a precipice, perhaps. Or a steep riverbank. The water here in the valley of shadows and darkness foams and roars, laced by jagged rocks. Passing through a deep and narrow gorge, we perhaps press ourselves hard against battlements of rock and sheer walls of stone.

These are words that describe the valleys—or *wadis*—so familiar to Palestine, the Holy Land, the setting of Psalm 23. It's wilderness, dear one. I know, for I've seen it and walked it myself. It's desert...where there are pits, ravines, and caves, the dryness of drought and the shadow of death. It's truly a no-man's land, a terrain that signals both danger and death.

Just one reading through the Old Testament will reveal 18 uses of the term "shadow of death." It means darkness, deep darkness, *very* deep darkness, thick darkness, and a darkness as dark as death. (Are you getting the picture?!) Its meaning includes the "death shadow" and the extreme dangers of the desert where death is dominant because the desert is a place of death.

∾ ✤ ∾

## ∾ *Reflecting on God's Promises* ∾

Have you, precious friend, ever traveled down, down, down into any dark valleys yourself? Can you remember a time of foreboding or panic? Of suffering and sorrow? Of terror as darkness seemed to overshadow you and swallow you up as you journeyed into the unknown?

I can pinpoint a few personal dark times myself.

❧ Five years of wanting children and not being able to have any.

❧ Ten days beside my father-in-law's deathbed.

❧ Three days beside my mother-in-law's deathbed (and without Jim!).

❧ One year of watching my father decline and die.

ᔰ The beginning months on the mission field—a stranger in a strange land.

ᔰ Several "mothering" times when things didn't seem to be going in the right direction.

ᔰ A battery of tests for cancer.

Yes, I've known the darkness. I've tasted the fear. But, beloved, I can now praise God for those dark times. Why? Because I now know something of His promised presence—He was there with me, and because I now know something of His grace—it was sufficient for me in those terrifying times. His gracious presence enabled me to journey *through* those valleys of darkness and death. As David, the psalmist, wrote, "Yea, though I walk *through* the valley of the shadow of death...."

Perhaps even now you face the downward path of darkness or are in the valley of the shadow of death. The day that I taught this powerful verse at our women's Bible study, I jotted down just four of the prayer requests for the day: One woman was facing her own battery of physical examinations for an unknown malady; another had just lost a ten-year-old child through death; one of our missionaries was suffering physically on the field, where there was a lack of medical care; and another dear lady had a setback in her cancer treatment. This list represents *one* day and *one* group of women! Oh, how many more there are who walk in darkness!

It's true that the perilous valley is a part of life's path. Yes, life includes the dangers and shadows of chronic illness and pain, of loss of finances and security, of aging, of medical tests and treatments, of surgeries with unknown futures on the other side, of repairing from the loss of someone near and dear to you, of suffering with one you love but cannot help.

But it's also true that we can grasp the hand of God as we descend the frightening path into the valley, into the devouring darkness. We can rest in the knowledge that He, this path, has already trod. And we are to walk...calmly...with Him...remembering the words, "Yea, though I *walk...*"

So *walk,* dear suffering one! Never fail to walk and to keep on walking! Don't pause. Don't falter. Don't ponder. Just proceed. Walk! Know that as the Shepherd's dear sheep and as God's beloved child and with the Lord beside you, you will walk *through* it. It comforts the soul to know that the Good Shepherd does not take His sheep into the valley of darkness to stay—but to pass *through* it. "Yea, though I walk *through* the valley of the shadow of death..."

## *The Walk in the Path*

Wow! All seems dark, doesn't it? Everything seems hopeless down in the valley, doesn't it?

But David did not end his verse nor his psalm *in* the valley of the shadow of death. Nor do we stop and stay there in its foreboding darkness. Neither David's psalm nor this book are meant to discourage the Lord's sheep. Oh, no! Quite the opposite! For, you see, every shadow is produced by light. It is impossible to have a shadow without a light.

And, dear one, our Lord *is* light! And He, the light of this world (Psalm 36:9 and John 1:4-9), has promised to be with us every step of the way. Indeed, *He* lights our path...one step at a time...one turn at a time.

That's how it was for the shepherds of old, and perhaps that's the image here. Those shepherds carried a lamp made out of parchment folded much like a Chinese lantern. After lighting the little oil lamp inside the lantern, the shepherd would hold it up high so that it would give light to his feet— one step at a time—as he led his sheep through the darkness—one step at a time.

~ ❧ ~

## ~ *Reflecting on God's Promises* ~

As you and I walk through our valleys of darkness, it's crucial to remember a handful of facts about God:

*Remember...we walk by divine appointment.* The valleys we enter are never accidental or the result of some mistake on God's part. No, we are *led* there by our all-wise, all-knowing, all-powerful Lord Jehovah. For He it is who knows the end from the beginning, the outcome of each and every pathway we tread. He it is who orders our steps (Psalm 37:23). As the Proverbs say,

∮ A man's heart plans his way, but the LORD directs his steps (Proverbs 16:9).

∮ A man's steps are of the LORD; how then can a man understand his own way? (Proverbs 20:24).

*Remember...we walk in divine presence.* No matter the twists and turns, the entanglements and obstacles along the path, "You are with me," David declares. We are never alone along the way. God is always with us. And He never fails.

I mentioned that I sat three days and nights beside my husband's dear mother Lois's bed when she was dying and Jim was away in Germany on an Army assignment. Late one night during my vigil (after midnight), the nurses encouraged me to go home and get some rest. Only after securing their promise to call if there was any change in Lois's condition did I leave her side. Two hours later the ringing phone jarred me out of my sleep. It was the hospital telling me that Lois had died. As I rushed to the car (I had slept in my clothes...just in case), I wept—not with sorrow, but with anger! What happened? Why hadn't they called? How could it be that Lois had died utterly alone?

But, oh, the precious assurance of Psalm 23:4—"Yea, though I walk through the valley of the shadow of death, I will fear no evil; for *You* are with me!" Oh, blessed assurance! And oh, blessed reminder! No, Lois hadn't been alone. She had been with her Friend who sticks closer than a brother (or a son or a daughter-in-law or a nurse or a doctor). She had been—and *was!*—with her Savior, her Shepherd, all the way. Indeed, she had never been out of His presence!

*Remember...we walk by divine grace.* We'll address the fear aspect of the valley of dark shadows in a minute, but for now just acknowledge that God has promised that His grace *is* and *will be* sufficient for all our needs (2 Corinthians 12:9). We experience fear when we try to imagine or anticipate future events. But the truth is that *when* we need God's marvelous grace, it will be there.

I love this story told by author Corrie ten Boom about wisdom passed on to her by her father. Corrie-the-child once worried out loud, "Daddy, I don't think I could suffer or be a martyr for Jesus Christ. My faith is not strong enough."

Her father patiently answered, "Corrie, when you go by train from Haarlem to Amsterdam, when do I give you the train ticket? Several days before?"

"No, Daddy, the day I go to travel."

"And so it is with God. Now you do not need the grace to suffer, but if the moment comes when you need it, He will give you the grace. He will give you the train ticket right on time."[1]

I'm sure these words—and God's great grace!—strengthened Corrie-the-prisoner as she suffered in a Nazi concentration camp during World War II!

*Remember...we walk by divine purpose.* And exactly what is the purpose (or at least one of them) of the valleys we must traverse? Why, it's intimacy with the Shepherd! Valleys are not meant to dishearten us or to provoke us or to trouble us. Valleys are merely passageways that bring us into greater closeness with our Lord. Just as we must go out into the dark night to behold the brilliance of the stars, so God's presence shines the brightest in our valleys of deep darkness.

So...walk slowly, dear pilgrim, when you walk through darkness and death. As one has noted, "It is a great art to learn to walk through the shadowy places. Do not hurry; there are lessons to be learned in the shadows that can never be learned in the light. You will discover something about God's ministries you never knew before. When we go into the valley of the shadow of death, we come so near Him that we look into His face and say not, "*He* is with me"—that is too formal, too far away—but "*You* are with me"![2] Oh, walk with Him *through* the dark valleys until you trust Him in the dark ever as much as you trust Him in the light!

# The "I Will" of the Path

As we step back into our Psalm, we next encounter one of David's greatest "I wills" in the Bible—"I will fear no evil."

And David had every opportunity to live in crippling fear! As a young teen he encountered lions and bears while watching over his father's flocks on the lonely and dangerous hillsides of Israel. He also confronted the giant, Goliath. As a man, David was misunderstood, falsely accused, and hunted down by Saul. He was forced out of his own home and city to live in the wilderness hiding out in caves. As a warrior, David led and fought in many a battle. As a shepherd, he also knew that fear is one of the great enemies of a flock of sheep, causing sheep to scatter and resulting in injury and even death. Oh, yes, David knew fear well!

But David also knew the Shepherd well. Thus David learned to face the tragedies and terrors of life *with* the Shepherd and therefore *without* fear. He boldly declared, "I will fear no evil." Why? Because of the presence of God—"*You* are with me."

We, too, my friend, are not to fear. And why? Because we, too, just like David, walk *with* our Lord. Whatever life brings, we will walk through it *with* the Shepherd, in His presence. Whatever losses we taste or stresses we bear, we will march through them *with* our Lord. Whatever enemies or threats to our life and loved ones we meet up with, we need not fear, for He is *with* us. He is, indeed, "a very present help in trouble. Therefore we will not fear..." (Psalm 46:1-2).

And just a factual note here, please, to assist us in achieving such fearlessness—more then 80 times in the Bible God tells us, "Fear not...!" Indeed, a frequent command issued by Jesus was, "Fear not." "Do not be anxious."

~ ❧ ~

# ~ *Reflecting on God's Promises* ~

Beloved, we are not to fear. Period! We are not to fear any thing, any human, any situation, any calamity, any possibility, any uncertainty, any season, or any loss. That's that! Any fear on our part signals loudly a lack of faith in our Lord... who is with us, through ev'ry day, o'er all the way.

And we are not to fear death. This chapter has been about walking through the valley of darkness, and, true, the reality of death is a portion of that walk in the valley. But, I repeat, you and I are not to be afraid, even though we walk through the valley of the shadow of death! And, again, why are we to be fearless? And the answer again is because our dear Shepherd has promised to be there, right there, *with* us!

*Learn about the Shepherd*—from the writer who expounded on these words regarding death: "How can *that* be dark, in which God's child is to have the accomplishment of the longing desire of his life? How can it be dark to come in contact with the light of life?"[3]

*Learn about the Shepherd*—from missionary Hudson Taylor's wife who uttered these words of encouragement to her dear grieving husband as she lay in her dying valley: "You know darling, that for ten years past there has not been a cloud between me and my Saviour.... I cannot be sorry to go to Him."[4]

As a sobering stanza of poetry declares,

> Afraid? Of what?
> To feel the spirit's glad release,
> To pass from pain to perfect peace,
> The strife and strain of life to cease—
> Afraid—of that?[5]

*Learn about the Shepherd*—from martyr John Stam who was beheaded with his wife in their valley, who wrote these words to family and friends as their situation in China darkened: "If we should go on before, it is only the quicker to enjoy the bliss of the Saviour's presence, the sooner to be released from the fight against sin and Satan."[6]

*Learn about the Shepherd*—from these words read at the funeral of my friend's dear mother-in-law: "Think...

...of stepping on a shore and finding it heaven;

...of breathing new air and finding it celestial air;

...of feeling invigorated and finding it immortality;

...of passing from storm and tempest to an unknown calm;

...of waking and finding it heaven;

...of taking hold of a hand and finding it the pierced hand of Jesus.[7]

And so, beloved...

*Sing*...as you pass onward through the valley of the shadow of death, and let the notes of your joy vibrate against the walls of that valley!

*Seek*...greater knowledge of the Lord, your Shepherd by faithfully acquainting yourself with His omnipotence and His omnipresence as revealed in His eternal Word!

*Step*...out in faith onto each and every path, knowing that "The Lord is my Shepherd—not *was*, not *maybe*, not *will* be. The Lord *is* my Shepherd, *is* on Sunday, *is* on Monday, *is* through every day of the week; *is* in January, *is* in December, and every month of the year; *is* at home, *is* in China; *is* in peace, and *is* in war; *is* in abundance and *is* in poverty. *The Lord is my Shepherd!*"[8]

∾ ∾ ∾ ∾ ∾ ❧ ∾ ∾ ∾ ∾ ∾

...and He is ever present with you!

# ~8~

# God's Promise of Comfort

~

*I will fear no evil; for You are with me;*
*Your rod and Your staff, they comfort me.*
PSALM 23:4

*Blessed be the God and Father*
*of our Lord Jesus Christ,*
*the Father of mercies and God of all comfort,*
*who comforts us in all our tribulation...*
2 CORINTHIANS 1:3-4

~

Take comfort! The Lord who is always present is there...
in the stillness beside a quiet stream...and in the shaking of
the mountains; at the hearth at home...and in the hospital;
in accusation...and in acquittal; in trial...and in triumph;
in pain...and in pleasure; in seasons of activity...and in aging;
in prison...and in paradise.
He is there when you pass through the waters...and
through the rivers...and through the fire!
—*Elizabeth George*

$\mathcal{W}$asn't it splendid to spend a chapter beholding the wonderful presence of our wonderful Lord? Oh, how blessed we are to dwell in the light of the presence of Him who knows our every movement, thought, and word, and is acquainted with all our ways! Truly, such knowledge is too wonderful for us! It is high, and we cannot comprehend it (see Psalm 139).

But, please, let's linger a little longer. Let's take in a little more about what the presence of the Lord should mean to us. Let's give a little more thought to the comfort we can enjoy in His company as we journey through the dark, threatening valley of shadows—or any other path where God chooses to lead us.

David wrote these promise-laden words: *I will fear no evil; for You are with me; Your rod and Your staff, they comfort me.* We know that David was not only a shepherd but also a warrior. And yet the warrior David is letting us know that he did not find his comfort in the dark and terrible times of battle from the weakness of his enemy nor in his own strength. No, he found comfort in the singular promise that the Lord was with him—fully armed with His rod and His staff!

As David writes the five words, "for You are with me," he speaks of the omnipresence of the Lord, the fact that God is always with us. And this thought brings us to another name of God. All along our walk through Psalm 23, we've been looking at some of the names of God that this beloved song seems to illustrate. And here in verse 4, we can't help but think of *Jehovah-Shammah*, meaning "Jehovah-is-there."

## *Jehovah Is There—Jehovah-Shammah*

As with the other names and characteristics of God that we've considered in this book, there's a history behind *Jehovah-Shammah*. And this assuring name of God comes to us out of the Old Testament book of Ezekiel. Here are a few facts to help our understanding:

- ⸔ Ezekiel was one of God's prophets who was taken as a captive to Babylon along with God's people (Ezekiel 1:1).

- ⸔ God asked Ezekiel to announce to the nation of Judah that they had been destroyed and removed from their homeland because of their sins (Ezekiel 2:5).

Talk about dark! Israel was at its lowest ebb ever in its history. And, due to their chastisement, God's people had finally gone from being stiff-necked and hardhearted to being broken in spirit. Where once they were proud and obstinate, they at last came to the place (away from their beloved homeland and as slaves to a foreign government) where they lived in humiliation and genuine sorrow for their sins. In fact, their sorrow was so deep that they could not even sing their beloved songs about the beauty of Zion, of Jerusalem, but instead hung their harps on the willow trees...and wept (Psalm 137).

Shooting across the dark skies that hovered over this scene of sorrow (truly a valley of darkness for God's people), came the dazzling promise of hope and consolation from God as spoken by Ezekiel: God would *restore* the land of Judah and *return* His people to it! And behold, as Ezekiel announced that when they finally arrived "home," Jehovah would be there, too! In *Jehovah-Shammah* (Ezekiel 48:35), we have God's promise of restoration, comfort, and hope. "The LORD is there!"

I know this name of God—*Jehovah-Shammah*, "the LORD is there"—sounds comforting and strengthening and evokes feelings of relief and reassurance. But there's more to it than mere emotion! You see, the uniqueness and glory of Israel's religion had always been the presence of God dwelling in their midst. Whether by the Angel of the Lord or the Shekinah glory dwelling in the cloud and the pillar of fire and in the tabernacle and temple of God, God was present with His people. He dwelt in a city—the City of God (meaning literally *Jehovah-Shammah,* The Lord is there)—and He was the Helper of His people. Away from Zion, the City of God, there was turmoil and tumult, war and ruin. But in Zion and with God there was safety, security, tranquility. Why? Because the Lord was there—*Jehovah-Shammah!*

I'm sure you can see why the Israelites longed to return to their homeland. The hope of God's presence was there!

~ ✹ ~

## ∼ *Reflecting on God's Promises* ∼

David realized the presence of God as he described "the valley of the shadow of death" and God's presence with him there. And, dear one, this is why you and I, too, as God's precious sheep, can walk through any and every dark valley without fear. Why should we fear if we walk in the presence of God, our Shepherd? Why should we fear if the Lord is there?

Let me share with you again one of my favorite promises in the Bible:

> God is our refuge and strength, a very present help in trouble. Therefore we will not fear, though the earth be removed, and though the mountains be carried into the midst of the sea; though its waters roar and be troubled, though the mountains shake with its swelling. Selah (Psalm 46:1-3).

How did this promise become a personal favorite? Well, I had memorized it because I loved its sentiment. I liked the "feeling" I experienced as I thought on the fact that my God is a very present help in trouble.

But then one day, January 17, 1994, the earth under me *did* move and the mountains around me *did* shake! That was the day of the devastating 6.8 Northridge, California, earthquake.

Northridge is just three miles from my home...and 52 people died that day.

A tremor is one thing, but a full-fledged earthquake is quite another! And an earthquake is one thing, but an earthquake at 4:31 A.M. in the dead darkness of night is quite another! And an earthquake experienced with someone else is one thing, but an earthquake at 4:31 A.M. in the dead darkness of night *alone* is quite another!

So, my friend, picture me and a killer 6.8 earthquake, at 4:31 A.M....alone. In the terror of that black night, I'm glad to report, verse 4 of Psalm 23 did come to me in my valley of darkness—*Yea, though I walk through the valley of the shadow of death, I will fear no evil; for You are with me.* I was there...*in* that valley—but so was *He!*

And as gigantic aftershocks rolled and roared through our area one after the other only minutes apart, causing still more devastation and terror in that physically black night (for electric power was out for miles), Psalm 46 also came to my rescue in a still small voice out of the recesses of my heart—*God is our refuge and strength, a very present help in trouble. Therefore we will not fear....*

I learned then and there, beloved, about the promised presence and comfort of the Lord. About *Jehovah-Shammah.* About the Lord who is always present. He is there...in the stillness beside a quiet stream...and in the shaking of the mountains; at the hearth at home...and in the hospital; in accusation...and in acquittal; in trial...and in triumph; in pain...and in pleasure; in seasons of activity...and in aging; in prison...and in paradise. He is there when you pass through the waters...and through the rivers...and through the fire (Isaiah 43:2). *Jehovah-Shammah!* He is there!

It is incredible to think that...

> Lord of all being! Throned afar,
> Thy glory flames from sun and star;
> Center and Soul of every sphere,
> Yet to each loving heart how near![1]

*You are with me.* How near! Therefore, we will not fear!

## Comfort Is There

*Yea, though I walk through the valley of the shadow of death....* Although the valley of darkness is one of God's paths, the trip through the valley is not very pleasant. It is a course of constant danger. There are crags and stones. There are extremes of cold and heat. There are desert and steep mountain trails. There are poisonous snakes there. There are vicious animals lurking along the way.

∾ ✤. ∾

## ∾ *Reflecting Briefly on God's Promises* ∾

As English clergyman F. B. Meyer wrote and reminds us, "If we've been told that we're supposed to be on a bumpy track, then every jolt along the way simply confirms the fact that we're still on the right road!"[2]

∾ ∾ ∾ ∾ ✤. ∾ ∾ ∾ ∾ ∾

But, dear one, again, take comfort! God, our Shepherd, is armed! Therefore as His darling sheep we need never fear, whether by day or by night. Why? Because two distinct implements are in the Shepherd's hand and they bring comfort to our hearts. *Your rod and Your staff, they comfort me.* You and I have the promise of divine comfort as we walk life's pathway.

## *The Rod Is There*

Let me describe the rod of a shepherd (I think it will make you feel more "comfort"-able!). It's an instrument that hangs by the shepherd's side or is sheathed in a long narrow pouch attached to his cloak. Most generally, it's made of oak and is about two feet long, coming from a carefully chosen straight young tree. After tearing up the oak tree, the bulb at the beginning of the root, which is about the size of a man's fist, is trimmed to make the head of a club. Next a hole is carved through the rod so it can be tied to the shepherd's belt or hang from his wrist like a riding whip. Sometimes two-inch metal spikes are driven into the club so that one blow with it can kill an attacking animal or snake.

Most of us know that sheep have no defenses. God didn't make sheep with claws, nor horns, nor speed, nor tusks, nor spines, nor shells, nor fangs. No, all that the poor sheep has for defense is the shepherd and his rod. Armed with this instrument of protection and death, the shepherd can lead his sheep through tall grass, swinging the club back and forth to frighten any enemies, and prepare the way for his sheep. And with his tool of defense, the shepherd can beat off the enemies of the flock—eagles, snakes, wild animals, mountain lions, bears, wolves, coyotes, even robbers.

~ ❧ ~

## ~ *Reflecting on God's Promises* ~

I have a true confession to make—sometimes I feel defenseless as a Christian woman, sort of like a sheep without claws, horns, speed, tusks, etc. While others may use their mouths and swing their "rights"—and even their fists!—around, God asks His women to put on a meek and quiet spirit. We're called to gentleness and submissiveness (1 Peter 3:4). God prizes graciousness and sweetness in us (Proverbs 11:16).

But as our Psalm says, *Your rod and Your staff, they comfort me.* I can take comfort in the promise that *God* will take care of me. He will always come to my rescue when I need Him. He will also guide me with His wisdom. The Lord is always there, and He it is who will tread down my enemies! Ponder just a few of my favorite promises to us, dear sister. I've added my own emphasis to each to help bring out their promises. Hopefully they will comfort your heart as they do mine:

§  *He* shall bring forth your righteousness as the light, and your justice as the noonday (Psalm 37:6).

§  I will cry out to God Most High; to God who performs all things *for* me (Psalm 57:2).

§  Through God we will do valiantly, for it is *He* who shall tread down our enemies (Psalm 60:12).

§  I will be with him in trouble; *I* will deliver him... (Psalm 91:15).

§  If I say, "My foot slips," Your mercy, O LORD, *will* hold me up (Psalm 94:18).

§  *The* LORD will perfect that which concerns me (Psalm 138:8).

## The Staff Is There

Not only does God defend us—He also directs us. He not only protects us—He also points out the way. How? "Your rod and Your *staff*, they comfort me."

And what exactly is the shepherd's staff? It's a much longer stick than the rod, more like six feet in length. It enables the shepherd to climb up and over rocks to survey their stability before leading his sheep there. With his staff, a shepherd can check out crevices and caves for snakes and scorpions that could harm his sheep. And his staff is also used to prod loitering sheep and to separate those that are fighting.

A shepherd's staff also has a crook on one end, much like the end of a curved walking stick. For centuries, the staff with its crook has been used as an instrument of guidance and restraint, and has come to symbolize the wise control of a shepherd over his sheep. For instance, the crook can be slipped around a sheep's neck to restrain it or to guide it. The crook can also keep a sheep from falling. And this marvelous device is also wielded to rescue sheep. If a sheep falls, the shepherd can twist the crook until it hooks into the sheep's wool and then lift the sheep until it is once again on sure footing.

Oh yes, the staff is most invaluable to the shepherd as he cares for his flock. He can use it to draw the flock together and to keep them from wandering. He can use it to restore the little lambs to their ewes. He can count each sheep when night falls by gently tapping each one on the head with the staff as it enters the sheepfold. And the shepherd uses his staff to communicate with his sheep as they trek and amble along their many paths together. A touch of the staff becomes a gesture of intimacy while walking, even though the shepherd towers over the sheep.

And yes, the staff is also used to coax the sheep to follow. For instance, a tap on a back leg brings a sheep into position, and a tap on the head of the lead sheep makes it lie down so that the others will follow.

## ∾ *Reflecting on God's Promises* ∾

Hear now these fine words from one of God's sheep:

Regrettably, we do not always follow our Lord. Sometimes our zeal tapers. The flame of our passion for Christ burns low. We grow cold in heart. Prayer becomes a burden rather than a pleasure. Zest for Bible reading dwindles while zeal to win lost souls to Christ disappears. [We] drift into spiritual slumps. But praise God, He understands! His love will not let us go. Though we find ourselves wandering from His side, suddenly we feel the staff of His love tugging at our hearts.[3]

Oh, the touch of the Shepherd's staff! How we should welcome it...even yearn for it! And, oh, how it should comfort us! It is proof of His presence and proof of His everlasting love. In Him is comfort as He touches us and guides us and cares for us with His staff.

And now, dear friend, before we turn our thoughts forward and move on to other powerful promises from Psalm 23, please review these "Five Steps for Successfully Handling Sorrow":

Remember the place—*the valley of the shadow of death.*
Remember the proclamation—*I will fear no evil.*
Remember God's presence—*for You are with me.*
Remember God's protection —*Your rod and Your staff.*
Remember God's promise—*they comfort me.*

## ~9~

# God's Promise of Friendship

~

*You prepare a table before me...*
*You anoint my head with oil; My cup runs over.*
PSALM 23:5

*But there is a friend*
*who sticks closer than a brother.*
PROVERBS 18:24

~

In the midst of affliction my table is spread;
With blessings unmeasured my cup runneth o'er;
With perfume and oil thou anointest my head;
Oh, what shall I ask of Thy providence more?
—*J. Montgomery*

In our Father's house we can
come in from the cold...to the heat of a hearth.
Come in from loneliness...to fellowship.
Come in from war...to peace.
Come in from darkness...to light.
Come in from danger...to safety.
Come in from famine...to feast.
Come in from enmity...to friendship.
—*Elizabeth George*

*I*magine a scene like this...

You're in a desert. You're a fugitive. You're hot and panting as you flee for your life, pursued and hunted by the forces of a fierce enemy. At last you see a tent. Desperate, you run toward it, exhausting your final ounce of energy. Finally you touch the tent rope, dare to lift the flap...and suddenly as you enter you realize you're "the guest of honor." And, as a guest, you are safe!

Now imagine David, who had spent many of his days and nights being pursued by his enemies, as the painter of this friendly picture. In Psalm 23, verse 5, he writes—*You prepare a table before me in the presence of my enemies; You anoint my head with oil; My cup runs over.* We've already learned that on more than one occasion, David's life was at risk. And a quick review reveals some of these incidents.

As a young shepherd, David fought not only with lions and bears but also against the giant, Goliath.

As a servant to King Saul, David experienced many a murderous attempt on his life from the hands of the very man he served.

As a warrior, David fought and slew his "ten thousands" (1 Samuel 18).

After his wife Michal (Saul's daughter) helped him escape from King Saul's house, David spent the next several years fleeing from Saul's rage.

Seeking food, shelter, and a sword, David escaped to the priestly outpost of Nob.

David then ran to the King of Gath to avoid death at the hands of the Philistines.

As an "outlaw," David headquartered in a cave in the wilderness. There in that wild and mountainous region, David was hunted like the animals that lived there.

Even as the King of Israel, David was forced to flee for his life into the desert—from his own son!

It was this David, David the fugitive, who wrote of finding a gracious host, sumptuous provision... and a friend!... while being a victim on the run.

∾ ✄ ∾

## ∾ *Reflecting on God's Promises* ∾

Our experiences with flight and persecution may not be nearly as literal or dreadful as David's were, but we do have our bouts with enemies. There are those who make our life difficult, who hound us, who block us, who slander us, who delight in our demise, who persecute us. There are those who let us have it, who take up an active cause against us, who harass, browbeat, pick, and nag. There are those whose mission seems to be creating tension for us, making sure that we never relax.

I never fail to think of dear Hannah, a woman from the Bible (see 1 Samuel 1), who experienced firsthand the promise and reality of God's friendship. Childless and relentlessly provoked by her husband's other wife, Hannah had nowhere to turn. Yes, Hannah certainly fell into the category of one who was mercilessly persecuted by an enemy, an adversary, a rival, one who chided and taunted her year after year, scoffing and laughing at her barrenness.

But when Hannah went up to the house of the Lord to worship, she, as it were, lifted the tent flap...and entered into the presence and provision of the Lord. There in Shiloh, she poured out her problems and woes to Jehovah, a Friend who sticks closer than a brother (and in Hannah's case, a husband!). In God's presence, there was rest, there was camaraderie, there was help, and there was healing. Hannah left that place repaired, replenished, and rapturous!

You, too, have a friend in the Lord God who provides solace for you from your enemies and your problems. You, too, can enter into the presence of the One who provides a haven of rest while you are on the run. Do you need a visit with Him now? Just lift the tent flap...and delight yourself in the Lord and in His friendship!

∾ ∾ ∾ ∾ ∾ ✶ ∾ ∾ ∾ ∾ ∾

## The Server

Did you notice a change in language as we stepped into verse five? Just as the scenery for a stage play is changed between acts, there's a change of scenery here in Psalm 23. A new image is introduced in this verse, an image of a host and his guest. And suddenly we move from journeying *with* the Lord our Shepherd out in the wilderness and fields as He leads us as a sheep...to a scene of gracious hospitality and friendship *inside* His tent or home. The setting shifts to show the psalmist as a guest of honor, enjoying the warm hospitality that is so characteristic of the Middle East where Psalm 23 was written. Suddenly the shepherd-and-sheep imagery is replaced by one of human intimacy—by one of feasting and friendship.

Furthermore, our psalm is progressing. Have you followed the progression? In verse four we moved closer to God in intimacy, realizing His divine protection through dark times in the valley of darkness—even the darkness of death. We learned we could exclaim while in that valley, "You are with me!" We experienced the nature and extent of Jehovah's protection and comfort.

But now in our current verse, you and I are invited to focus on the promise of His protection and the blessings of His friendship: *You prepare a table before me in the presence of my enemies. You anoint my head with oil; my cup runs over.* All along the way we've needed God's protection, guidance, and provision. But here we experience the lavishness of His friendship as well.

## The Supply

David writes, *You prepare a table before me.* We've seen who our host and server is—it's the Lord Himself! But now we're allowed to see the supply our Host has heaped upon His table.

And it's truly a sight to behold! Oh, the labor! And, oh, the work that's gone into spreading such a feast! You see, the table is *prepared*...prepared for you. You're not an unexpected guest, but an anticipated one. You're not a drop-in guest, but an invited one. This is not a quick snack where something (or some leftovers!) was thrown together, but one where preparations were carefully made in advance. No, the table is elaborately furnished and literally and liberally spread with food!

Truly, this scene is a prototype of the table furnished by the wise woman from Proverbs 9:2 and of the ultimate, great table prepared by Christ for His bride (Revelation 19:9)!

∾ ✢ ∾

## ∾ *Reflecting on God's Promises* ∾

As a friend of God, my fellow traveler, you and I never have to worry about God's provision. As David declared previously, *I shall not want.* When God elects to feed a soul, then fed that soul shall be! No, the time can *never* come when God's table is bare. Indeed, God can furnish a table and give a banquet in the desert (Psalm 78:19)!

I recently read about a couple who announced to their families that they were no longer going to "do" Christmas, Thanksgiving, Easter, or birthdays, citing grocery shopping, cooking, and family dinners as a pain. Instead they were opting for sitting on the sofa with a stack of books and relaxing in front of the VCR with a dozen or so movies. The preparations and time for family gatherings were written off as a waste!

But, dear child of God, *He* prepares a table for you and me! He prepares His best. And He prepares what is best for us as we walk and wade through life. And He also prepares in advance, sets His banqueting table, and waits for us weary traveling friends to lift the tent flap...and allow Him to minister to us. The thought of such lavish love can at times (depending on how tired or how wounded I am) move me to tears. This, precious one, is *our* God, the One who prepares a table in the wilderness for us when we are wasted and worn—and worn out!

And, by the way, as the "server" in your home, are you supplying a table for those in your dear family and within your sphere of ministry? Are you pouring your love into gracious and generous preparations for your own precious weary and worn-out family members? Is your table set? Prepared? Furnished? Spread out with the nourishment needed to sustain their work and the battles they each must fight? We have the privilege of providing for those we love— just like our heavenly Father provides for us. And *He* prepares a table before us!

# The Style

Before we look at the protection our Sovereign supplies to His guests, let's finish our time at His table and notice the style with which He serves His friends. There are two additional marks of His hospitality and friendship and generosity toward His weary people.

*First, the anointing of the head.* In the words of David, *You anoint my head with oil.* (Oh the lavishness of our holy Host! He not only feeds us, but he anoints us, too!) In yet another gracious gesture, He anoints the head of His guest with perfumed oil. This is a blatant act of luxury—for oil is costly. It's also a symbol of festivity—for the oil of joy always replaces mourning (Isaiah 61:3). And it's a sign of happiness—for ointment and perfume rejoice the heart (Proverbs 27:9).

Chemists tell us of three unique pleasures and distinct qualities of oil:

> Touch—oil provides a smoothness.
> Sight—oil gives a brightness.
> Smell—oil supplies a fragrance.

All three elements combined gratify the senses and are sources of delight to the one anointed. Imagine the running and hounded traveler...treated to something so gladdening out of the bounty of a friendly, generous host!

*Second, the filling of the cup.* David adds, *My cup runs over.* The magnitude of God's provision includes the well-filled cup. This is the cup used for drinking liquid at a dinner or banquet. Large and deep, its contents were meant to satisfy the thirst, refresh the body, and invigorate the soul. Filled to overflowing—that's what the cup of God's guest is! And the one fortunate enough to drink from it will be filled and saturated.

Indeed, as with all of God's other provisions for us as His beloved friends, the cup, too, is full and complete, brimming until it spills over.

∾ ✣ ∾

## ∾ *Reflecting on God's Promises* ∾

There's no doubt about it—our Lord's provision for us as His friends represents thoughtfulness and excess. As we tiredly and frantically enter into the refuge of His tent in the desert, as we draw up the tent-flap and behold the treasure of His table—a table prepared and filled and waiting for us—we see plenty of necessary food. But, dear one, there's also the oil of His joy and the filling of our cup to measures above and beyond! We're truly stunned by God's abundance (not to mention His abundant goodness to us!).

The sustenance, the oil, and the brimming cup do their job well and revive us. They simultaneously brace us, stimulate us, and delight us! They truly turn our time at God's table into a festival of joy!

When we think of all the riches of grace which we have in our Lord God, we should burst forth with the grateful acknowledgment, *My cup runs over!* As one has written,

> Nothing narrow, nothing stinted
> Ever issues from God's store;
> To His own He gives full measure,
> Running over evermore.[1]

# *A Sample of Blessings*

How blessed we are, dear one, to be called "friend" by the Sovereign God of the universe! Just think about it! Our divine Host is the awesome, all-powerful, all-knowing, always-present One. And yet, we discover, He is also our Friend. And before we move on from this overwhelming (not to mention humbling!) thought, I want us to pause and consider just a sample of the many blessings that you and I discover in God's friendship right here in verse five. Spend just a few moments marveling at all that a visit with your friendly Host promises to be....

## ∾ *Ten Reflections on God's Promises* ∾

1. *Increased intimacy*—It's one thing to be a sheep with the Shepherd. But it's quite another to be a guest in His home! In our Father's house there is fullness of joy and pleasures forevermore (Psalm 16:11).

2. *Divine care*—Jehovah's care for you and me is expressed in the fact that He Himself prepares a table for us. Imagine the joy of feasting in God's presence, at His table, and on the fare from His hand! Truly, we shall not want!

3. *Gracious amenities*—God, our heavenly Host, anoints your head with oil and fills your cup to overflowing. We can declare along with David, "Who am I, O LORD

God...that You have brought me this far?" (2 Samuel 7:18).

4. *A haven in a hostile world*—The psalmist speaks of enemies, but no enemy can come so near that God is not nearer! No matter where we roam, and no matter how many enemies pursue, and no matter how hard the path, we need only lift His divine tent flap...and enjoy a retreat for our soul! All who find their refuge in the Lord find not only a Friend but rest, refreshment, relaxation, renewal, and revival.

5. *A shelter from the storms of life*—In our Father's house we can come in from the cold...to the heat of a hearth. Come in from loneliness...to fellowship. Come in from war...to peace. Come in from darkness...to light. Come in from danger...to safety. Come in from famine...to feast. Come in from enmity...to friendship.

6. *A warm welcome*—As we arrive, we find we are expected. We've been anticipated. We're greeted. Preparations have been made in advance. Our host has been waiting to wrap His arms around us in friendship.

7. *A place to pause*—As we run from place to place, event to event, we can always halt in our Host's home. We stop. We

breathe. We pause. We enjoy. We sup. We rest. We fellowship. We regroup. In God's presence is heaven on earth!

8. *A hospital*—As we arrive weary and worn, haggard and breathless, battered and bruised, bleeding and terrorized, our heads are anointed and our wounds are bathed with the oil of healing.

9. *A generous heart*—In the intimacy of His house, our Host hovers over us, watching for any opportunity to provide magnanimously for us, continually refilling our cup as we drink from its lip. He delights in pouring out a generous portion.

10. *The blessings of friendship*—Here our Host is a picture of true concern, of society and fellowship, of all that comes from the heart of a true friend—the lavishness of the oil of joy and the cup filled with blessings of every kind. God is our promised Friend.

It's absolutely true—as Psalm 23 promises, the Lord always meets the needs of His people!

> He spread'st a table in my sight,
> Thy boundless grace bestoweth;
> And O! What transport of delight
> From Thy pure chalice floweth![2]

# ~ 10 ~

# God's Promise
# of Protection

~

*...in the presence of my enemies.*
PSALM 23:5

*O LORD my God, in You I put my trust;*
*Save me from all those who persecute me;*
*And deliver me.*
PSALM 7:1

*My times are in Your hand;*
*Deliver me from the hand of my enemies;*
*And from those who persecute me.*
PSALM 31:15

~

Our enemies have no power because
Our sovereign, all-powerful God controls the universe—
and that includes controlling those who are our enemies.
They cannot frustrate God's good plan or
His promised protection and victory!
—*Elizabeth George*

*I* still vividly remember one of those you-could-hear-a-pin-drop moments. It was on a Sunday morning, and our congregation was utterly silent as our pastor told a story about a missionary to cannibals. It seems that this dear man's wife had died on the ship carrying the couple to their new mission station. When the boat finally docked, the bereaved husband buried his wife on the shore of his new outpost and camped out for several days and nights beside his wife's grave to guard her body from the cannibals.

Later, when he began his ministry, and contact was established with the islanders, the heathen cannibals approached him with a question. They had watched the forlorn missionary as he'd stood vigil over his wife's grave, and they wanted to know, "Who were those men with you on the shore?" It seems that as the cannibals stalked the area, they'd kept their distance because the missionary was ringed by guards.

"Who *were* those men...?" Perhaps in heaven we'll find out!

But, my friend, our Bible is full of promises for God's protection. And it's also full of incidents of God protecting His people when they were in the presence of their enemies. It's just as David, the author of Psalm 23 and writer of the words in verse five about being *in the presence of my enemies,* says: "The angel of the LORD encamps all around those who fear Him, and delivers them" (Psalm 34:7)! For instance...

One ordeal in the Bible shows us a hopeless (*seemingly* hopeless, that is!) situation for one of God's prophets. Elisha and his servant were surrounded by horses and chariots and a great host of warriors who came in the night and circled the city where they were. When Elisha's servant saw the armed mass, he cried out to Elisha, "Alas, my master! What shall we do?"

Elisha, ever the man of faith, calmly replied, "Do not fear; for those who are with us are more than those who are with them."

And then Elisha prayed, "LORD, I pray, open his eyes that he may see."

And the Lord opened the eyes of the young man, and he saw; and, behold, the mountain was full of horses and chariots of fire round about Elisha (2 Kings 6:13-17). God's protection completely surrounded Elisha!

It's true, dear one. Out of His awesome power, God protects His people!

Now...back to the situation in Psalm 23....

## *The Situation*

Before we go on to enjoy more of God's promised protection, I want us to remember the scene of Psalm 23, verse five. In the last chapter, we looked at the friendship we enjoy with God. We marveled at His sumptuous provision of food, oil, and wine. And now we note the unique situation in which His bounty is provided—it is *in the presence of our enemies!*

Remember, too, that this was written by David whose life was filled with flight, fear, and reliance upon the hospitality of others. Not only did David experience the enemies of the wilderness (beasts, scorching heat, and lack of water), but he also had enemies on two legs—robbers, warriors, armies, and upstart rulers! Yet many times, as a young boy, as a warrior, and as a king, David found himself dining...in the presence of his enemies.

## *The Scene*

In our hurry-up lifestyle of meet-you-at-the-restaurant dinners and drive-thru eat-it-on-the-go lunches, it's hard for us to envision the scene the psalmist is sketching for us in verse five of dining in an Eastern culture—although it be in a tent!

*A scene of warm hospitality*—We've already considered the abundant provision of the prepared and lavishly furnished table, the anointing oil, and the running-over cup. No, I repeat, we can't imagine what it was like to be a guest in those ancient times. But we can read in the Bible about Abraham and Sarah rushing to select and prepare the very best food available for their three guests (Genesis 18). In those days of traveling on foot and on beast, and in that land of desert, wilderness, and extreme heat and cold, travelers depended on the provision of strangers to keep them alive. It was a way of life.

## ∼ *Reflecting on God's Promises* ∼

I hope you'll take advantage of the many books available to us about Christian hospitality. And I hope you're developing a heart that desires to invite others to your home—those you know and love, those who live around you, those you do not know, and those who are needy. It sounds unspiritual, but we must *choose* to nurture a heart of hospitality. Somehow we seem to think it will just happen, that it comes with being a Christian. But the truth is that we must cultivate it. So, I'm suggesting that we begin the nurturing process.

> Pick a time.
> Invite some guests.
> Plan a menu.
> Involve the family.
> Prepare in advance.
> Pray about the event.
> Be faithful and follow through.

Just this morning, my husband, Jim, announced that the missions board at our church (and Jim is on that board) wanted each board member to have our furloughing missionaries into our homes once a month. And so Jim and I sat down, calendars in hand, and picked the dates and the time, talked through a simple, do-able menu, and planned the flow of the

> evenings—beginning and ending times, the serving of the dinner, and a time of sharing and prayer.
>
> Beloved, as you develop a heart of hospitality and open your home to others, you're in for a double blessing! Your guests will be blessed ...and so will you!

≈ ≈ ≈ ≈ ≈ ✄ ≈ ≈ ≈ ≈ ≈

*A scene of security*—And now we move from friendship to protection (which is what this chapter is about). You see, Eastern hospitality is synonymous with protection, because to be someone's guest meant to be safe...at least for the duration of the stay inside the host's home! Therefore, dining, especially in the presence of enemies, denotes a sense of security. Why? Because the host was obliged to protect his guests...at any cost.

One particular scene in the Bible shows us vividly this duty to protect one's guests. Abraham's nephew, Lot, protected his guests in Genesis 19. In this frightening scene, Lot not only served his guests a feast but he also shielded them from the pressing mob gathered at his door.

Another instance illustrates the duty...in reverse! It has to do with two brothers. One brother, Solomon, was not invited to a feast held by his brother Adonijah. Why? Adonijah planned to kill Solomon. And under the code of Eastern hospitality, Adonijah would be obligated to protect Solomon if he came to eat with him. Therefore, Adonijah did not invite Solomon to his feast (1 Kings 1).

Yes, to be a guest meant to be protected.

*A scene of victory*—Another Eastern custom is portrayed as David speaks of dining *in the presence of my enemies*. In David's day, enemies who were conquered in battle were forced to watch the victory celebration. Sometimes a prisoner was chained to each pillar of the palace in order to "feast" his eyes on the victory feast. The scene went something like this: The enemies, present as captives, watched, up close and personal, the banqueting victors eat to their hearts' content while the prisoners of war went without.

∾ ❦ ∾

## ∾ *Reflecting on God's Promises* ∾

Our enemies...sigh! I've been reading through the Psalms again. And I was hit again by how much of David's poetry centers on his bouts with his enemies. He moans to God with words to this effect, "O Lord! I have so many enemies! How long will they ruin my reputation? They maul me like a lion! Lord, have mercy on me. See how I suffer at the hands of those who hate me!" (see Psalms 3,4,7,9).

Our enemies...sigh again! They seem to be a fact of life. But we are not to hate them. We are not to fight them. We are not to fear them. We are not to fret or worry about them. And we are not to envy them.

Instead, we are to do as David did and *cry out to God*. We are to pray *for* them. We are to pray *about* them.

And we are also to *count on God's promises*. He promises to bring forth our righteousness as the light...therefore we are not to fret...(Psalm 37:6-7). He promises to avenge us. And He promises to protect us. Our sovereign, all-powerful God controls the universe—and that includes controlling those who are our enemies. Compared to God, our enemies have no power. They cannot frustrate God's good plan or His promised protection and victory.

Yes, we live in the midst of deadly enemies. And yes, they can make our life miserable. But, dear one, they cannot have the victory! Ever! We will safely feast in the presence of our enemies—and in spite of our enemies! It's a promise!

## The Savior—Jehovah-Nissi

God's protection of us as His people and His provision for our every need—even in the presence of our enemies!—is a staggering promise. And there's another reason we need never worry about God's protection. He protects us as a savior because He is *Jehovah-Nissi,* meaning "the LORD is my banner."

As we've seen with the other names of God mentioned in this book, there's an exciting background for this name, too. We find its appearance in the book of Exodus, chapter 17.

It all began as God's people wandered in the wilderness. When the Amalekites attacked them, Moses, their leader, went into action. Here's a quick summary of the story:

*First,* Moses appointed Joshua to lead Israel into battle.

*Second,* Moses assured Joshua that he would stand on top of a hill with his staff, the rod of God, in his hand. While

Moses' staff was lifted into the air, the battle went well, and, in the end, Joshua won the clash.

*Third,* Moses built an altar to celebrate Israel's victory and named the altar *Jehovah-Nissi,* meaning "The LORD is My Banner" (Exodus 17:15).

The name Moses chose, *Jehovah-Nissi,* revealed Israel's confidence that God was the One who gave them the victory. It was also a reminder that God was the One they should rally around as their banner in future skirmishes.

You see, a banner (also called a standard or ensign) was simply a bare pole with a bright ornament on the top. This ensign would glisten and shine in the sun. In fact, the word in Hebrew means "to glisten." At the time of the battle with the Amalekites, the banner was the rod of God, Moses' staff. Later, in another crisis, Moses lifted up a pole topped with a bronze emblem of a serpent that saved the life of every Israelite who looked at it (Numbers 21:9).

With incidents like these, it's easy for us to understand how a "banner" or an emblem on a pole came to signify a miracle! A military word which stood for God's causes and God's battles, it carried a strong signal to the Israelites to rally to God. In our language, we might say, "Rally 'round the flagpole, boys!" Ultimately, it was a sign of deliverance and salvation, a sign of God's protection.

God's rod in Moses' hand on that victorious day became a symbol and a pledge of God's presence and power to His people *in the presence of their enemies.* Moses experienced *Jehovah-Nissi*—"The LORD is My Banner"—in the presence of Israel's enemies.

David, too, when he wrote these lines in Psalm 23, anticipated ultimate victory and deliverance *in the presence of his enemies* because he rallied under God's banner of protection in His home as His guest.

## ∾ *Reflecting on God's Promises* ∾

I repeat, dear one, you and I never have to worry about God's protection. I like this strong example of faith in *Jehovah-Nissi*'s protection from the life of Martin Luther. When making his way into the presence of an enemy, the Cardinal who had summoned him to answer for his heretical opinions, Luther was asked by one of the Cardinal's servants, "Where shall you find shelter if your patrons and protectors should desert you?"

Luther's answer? "Under the shield of heaven!"

Rejoice, beloved. *Always* rejoice...because *Jehovah-Nissi* is your banner, your protector, your rescuer, your deliverer, your shield, and your Savior.

So let's review. We've witnessed the situation—*the presence of enemies*. We've experienced the scene—the safety and protection of our divine Host. And we've beheld our Savior—*Jehovah-Nissi*, the LORD our Banner. Now, don't you think we're fully cared for and fully armed with the protection of our God? So...

§ As you face adversaries through life, remember: The ultimate victory is yours because of God's great power...even in the presence of your enemies.

§ As you rally under His name *Jehovah-Nissi* and look to Him and the standard of His banner, remember: You are protected...even in the presence of your enemies.

§ As you, in faith, lift up *Jehovah-Nissi* high in your heart, remember: Deliverance is yours...even in the presence of your enemies.

Beloved, if God is on our side, what does it matter who is against us?!

I've already shared from the hymn, "Like a River Glorious," but a few more of its moving words seem appropriate here as we're challenged to trust in God's promise to protect us.

Hidden in the hollow of His blessed hand,
never foe can follow, never traitor stand...
We may trust Him fully all for us to do—
They who trust Him wholly find Him wholly true.[1]

# ~ 11 ~

# God's Promise
# of Hope

~

*Surely goodness and mercy shall follow me
all the days of my life.*
PSALM 23:6

*Through the LORD's mercies we are not consumed,
Because His compassions fail not.
They are new every morning;
Great is Your faithfulness.*
LAMENTATIONS 3:22-23

~

…all the streams of goodness and mercy
flow freely from God's fountain—God's pardoning,
protecting, sustaining, and supplying goodness and mercy…
and they follow us as surely as the water out of
the rock followed Israel…
—*Matthew Henry*

Shouldn't the fact of God's promise of hope light a candle
in your heart and create a blaze of glorious hope
that dispels all darkness and doubt about the future?
Indeed, you and I face the unknown with The Known—
with the extended care of God, our Shepherd,
who is the same yesterday, today, and forever!
—*Elizabeth George*

$\mathcal{M}$y friend, as we enter this final verse of the Twenty-third Psalm, we must turn a corner in our faith. Like a ship setting out to sea, we must leave the familiar shore and all that is seen...and sail away on the winds of faith into the unseen. We must turn our focus away from looking at what we know to be true of God's past and present care for us...to looking at His promises to take care of us in the future. It will be quite a voyage—and a voyage of sheer faith!

But first, I want to tell you a story about "The Box."

One day a few years ago, I really had my eyes opened as to just how dependent I am on others (in this case, my husband!) for my financial needs. Jim and I were moving things out of our office to make way for some structural repairs (more earthquake damage!). As we came to a small metal box, I had to stop my packing. Its label, scrawled with a black marker on a strip of masking tape, simply read "Finances." Wondering what that could be, I undid the latch and peered into "The Box."

What I found inside that smallish grey box was humbling …and at the same time encouraging. In it was a bulging stack of receipts saved over the decades, proof of the payments Jim had been faithfully making into his retirement and pension plans. There lay the documents verifying his contributions to his medical and life insurance policies and to his social security account. Jim already provides for my everyday needs. But because of what's inside "The Box," his care for me will extend into the future. (As I said, it was humbling *and* encouraging!)

Now, my friend, whether we're married or single or young or old, verse six of Psalm 23 is like "The Box." It's a clear promise to you and me of God's provision for the future—*Surely goodness and mercy shall follow me all the days of my life.* Individuals can scheme and dream of ways to care for us…but God *can* and *will* care for us—every day. He will get the job done! It's a promise!

## *Looking Backward…and Upward*

Let's take a brief backward look at the Shepherd Psalm…and an upward look, too. I'm sure you've enjoyed many Fourth of July celebrations. You know well the thrill of the brilliant bursts and the booms and sizzles of exploding fireworks overhead. Well, looking backward at the profusion of promises God makes to us in Psalm 23 is like looking at a show of fireworks!

§ In verse 1—God promises us care and provision.
*The LORD is my shepherd; I shall not want.*

§ In verse 2—God promises us wisdom and daily bread.

*He makes me to lie down in green pastures; He leads me beside the still waters.*

§ In verse 3—God promises us guidance and restoration. *He restores my soul; He leads me in the paths of righteousness for His name's sake.*

§ In verse 4—God promises us companionship and comfort.
*Yea, though I walk through the valley of the shadow of death, I will fear no evil; for You are with me; Your rod and Your staff, they comfort me.*

§ In verse 5—God promises us safety, joy, and fellowship.
*You prepare a table before me in the presence of my enemies; You anoint my head with oil; my cup runs over.*

This expanse of God's promises makes it plain to see that God takes care of our every need throughout each and every day of life. He has in the past, and He does in the present.

But now, David, the author of our psalm, adds a new element of hope with an upward look—*Surely goodness and mercy shall follow me all the days of my life; and I will dwell in the house of the LORD forever.* Suddenly our walk with God, our Shepherd shifts...from the present tense (*is, makes, leads, restores,* You *are* with me, and they *comfort* me)...to the future tense (*shall* and *will*). And suddenly it becomes obvious that God plans and promises to take care of our every need in the future, too. Forever!

## ∾ *Reflecting on God's Promises* ∾

Before we move from experience to faith in our next section, I want us to move from "The Box" to "The Book." A rusty tin box filled with cracked, aging papers is one thing. But, dear friend, "The Book," the living Word of God, your Bible, is quite another! When it comes to promises for the future, "The Box" filled with insurance and asset papers may give you a little comfort along life's path. But the promises made in "The Book" will take you all the way through life—and beyond!

Did you know that estimations of the number of promises in the Bible range from 8,810 to 30,000?[1] While those to whom the promises were made are sometimes specific, there still remains an immeasurable number of promises that are shot directly from God's heart to yours. Therefore, be sure you pore over what's in "The Book" (and not what's in "The Box"!). Familiarize yourself with each and every word of your Bible. Handle and touch and count each and every priceless promise of hope. Treat them as pearls, as gems, as precious jewels, each one of them making you wealthy. Store them away as treasures but also wear them often. Memorize them and make them your own.

As one translator marvels, "Through [God's] might and splendour He has given us

His promises, great beyond all pric
1:4).[2] And, as King Solomon discover
self and passed on to us, "There ha
one word of all His good promise'
8:56).

~ ~ ~ ~ ~ ~ ~ ~ ~ ~

## *Moving from Experience to Faith*

*Surely!* David begins verse six with a profound "surely" (and I like to think that it's with a series of exclamation points!!!!!). He, too, is looking back at all that God has done and provided for him in the past, at how God has cared for his daily needs as they arose along the way...

...and with the word "surely," David does an about-face, turns around 180 degrees, looks his unknown future right in the face, and confidently declares, "Surely goodness and mercy shall follow me all the days of my life." With this statement, David moves from experience to faith. He knows he's under God's protection. His head is anointed with perfumed oil. His every need is completely satisfied. With faith and confidence building out of the lessons of the past, David feels that every moment of his future life will be filled with God's richest blessings, too. *Surely!!!!!*

As the sweet old hymn reminds us, God gives "strength for today and bright hope for tomorrow."[3] Well, dear friend, *hope* is what verse six is all about—hope for all our tomorrows. And for all the forever-days of our life!

~ ❧ ~

## ~ *Reflecting on God's Promises* ~

...all your tomorrows. As we pause here and dare to peek down the dark corridor of time-future, are your heart and mind filled with hope or with fear? Our natural tendency is to fear the unknown. What we don't know and don't understand generally bothers us.

When we look...

❦ *at our possessions* (Will there be another 6.8 earthquake, another Hurricane Andrew or Floyd, more flooding, blizzards, or power outages this year?),

❦ *at our families* (Will my children and/or grandchildren make wise decisions? Will they follow Christ?),

❦ *at our finances* (Will I have to get a job, keep working? Is there really enough money for retirement? Will my husband lose his job? Will I lose my husband?),

❦ *at our health* (Will the next physical exam reveal cancer...in me, in my husband? Will some disabling disease set in? Will there be years on end of suffering and pain?), and

§ at death (What will cause it? Wh
be like? What about my family?)

...we can easily wonder, "Is
hope?!"

But oh, beloved friend, that's exactly when
and where this precious promise of hope comes
to our rescue! Not only can David confidently
proclaim *Surely goodness and mercy shall follow
me all the days of my life,* but as God's precious
child, you can, too!

If you're not quite sure, just take an inven-
tory. Has the Lord faithfully and successfully
shepherded you in and through the past? Of
course! And will He faithfully and successfully
shepherd you in and through the future? Of
course! (Or as David affirms, *Surely!!!!!*) And
shouldn't God's promise light a candle in your
heart and create a blaze of glorious hope that
dispels all darkness and doubt about the future?
Indeed, you and I face the unknown with The
Known—with the extended care of God, our
Shepherd, who is the same yesterday, today, and
forever!

There's no need for you, as one of God's
cherished sheep and one of His own special
people, to ever lack hope! Oh, no! As His child,
you have His promised goodness and His promised mercy...all the days of your life!

# Seven Reasons for Hope in the Future—Part I

When Jim and I moved from Oklahoma to California, we took half a day out of our drive west to see the Grand Canyon. Oh, my! What a thrill! What a sight!

Well, you know the drill when you're in a National Park—you drive, stop, look, and take a picture. And that's what we did. We drove along the canyon rim, stopping at every viewing site of this vast canyon. Each time, we parked the car, got out, and took a short hike to a little lookout station. Out came the camera and Jim would take another photo of the canyon—but from a different angle than the last shot. On and on we drove, repeating our stop-hike-and-take-a-photo routine all the way along the canyon rim.

Well, that's the way I want us to look at verse six. Here we have seven shots, seven features, seven angles, seven different views of the same verse. We'll look at four of them here and save the final three for the next chapter. I think you'll find plenty of reasons for confidence and hope for your future. So prepare yourself for an even greater blessing than a feast abounding with food, oil, and the running-over cup. Prepare yourself for the goodness and mercy of the Lord!

## 1. God's Continued Goodness

Even though we've seen, tasted, and witnessed God's goodness for five verses (and ten chapters of this book!), what we see here in our first view of our hopeful future is God's *goodness*—"Surely [God's] *goodness*...shall follow me all the days of my life." And what is God's goodness? It is the sum total of all His attributes. When Moses asked to see God's glory, God answered, "I will make all My *goodness* pass before you" (Exodus 33:19, emphasis added). As another favorite Psalm simply remarks, "For the LORD is good" (Psalm 100:5).

God's goodness will follow and accompany us for the rest of our life.

## 2. *God's Continued Mercy*

The next stop on our tour of verse six is a look at the hope of God's mercy, which will also follow us all the days of our life. "Surely...[God's] *mercy* shall follow me all the days of my life." *Mercy* (or the wonderful, quaint old word *lovingkindness*) is David's word for God's tender affection. And its use in the ancient world meant love that flows, not out of a sense of duty, but from deep emotion. *Mercy* expressed God's steadfast love, even toward those who were unworthy and undeserving.

∾ ✻ ∾

## ∾ *Reflecting on God's Promises* ∾

The life of Rahab, a woman of the Bible, offers us one of God's most dramatic cameos displaying the light of His mercy against the background of dark, sinful deeds. Rahab was a woman who had every reason to be shunned and condemned by God and His people. Rahab, you see, was a harlot, a prostitute. Yet she had heard of God, feared the Lord, hid His spies, and helped them to escape death. As the spies from the army of Israel ran for their lives, they promised this dear woman who had risked her life that they would spare her and all her family when they came to conquer the land (Joshua 2).

Did this blatant sinner deserve to be spared? Did this woman who had broken God's holy Law merit even a drop of God's grace? Did this harlot warrant any special treatment or consideration from God and His people?

No.

And, my friend, neither do we! That's what makes Rahab's story so beautiful and touching. God says "there is none who does good, no, not one....for all have sinned and fall short of the glory of God...[and] the wages of sin is death" (Romans 3:12,23; 6:23).

But God...in His great mercy...extended His loving-kindness to the undeserving and unworthy sinner Rahab. In His compassion and grace, He saved her and her family, turning her dark life and sinful past into an exquisite cameo of shining faith.

Are you God's child, precious reader? Have you admitted your sins to a holy God? And have you asked for His mercy and forgiveness? Can you cry out with the tax collector in Luke 18:13, "God be merciful to me a sinner!"? If so, you have the promise and the hope of God's mercy...which shall *surely* follow you all the days of your life! Behold, the goodness and mercy of the Lord!

～ ～ ～ ～ ～ ❊ ～ ～ ～ ～ ～

## 3. *God's Continued Pursuit*

You and I probably have neither the knowledge nor the vocabulary to understand military subjects and references. But the writer of Psalm 23 was a warrior. David knew all about armies and forces and battles and warfare. And here in verse six, we witness David dipping into his military vocabulary bag and selecting a war-word to describe God's promise to take care of us all the days of our life. David writes, "Surely goodness and mercy shall *follow* me all the days of my life."

The picture the poet is painting with the word "follow" is one of pursuit, of being relentlessly pursued. Most of David's adult life was spent being pursued by his enemies and by the enemies of God. And now David puts this term to a more positive use, conveying that God's goodness and mercy will pursue us and "hound" us each and every day of our life, just as it had for David.

## 4. *God's Continued Presence*

Let's take just one more "snapshot" on our trip through the awesome verse six of Psalm 23 before this chapter ends. And that picture is of the hope we should experience because of the continued presence of the Lord. David says, "Surely goodness and mercy shall follow me *all the days of my life.*"

As David ponders the goodness and mercy of God, he gives them each a personality, a presence. He pictures them as following us, as shadowing us, as attending us, as hounding us, and as assuring us...that no matter what happens in our lives, today, tomorrow, or in all the todays that follow tomorrow, God's mercy and love will be there, too. They will *always* be there! No, nothing can ever separate us from God's goodness and mercy.

## ∾ *Reflecting on God's Promises* ∾

There are many illustrations of what these two attributes of God—His goodness and His mercy—might represent to us. But I liked this image and its devotional language best.

These two angels of God—Goodness and Mercy—shall follow and encamp around the pilgrim. The white wings of these messengers of the covenant will never be far away from the journeying child, and the air will often be filled with the music of their comings, and their celestial weapons will glance around him in all the fight, and their soft arms will bear him up over all the rough ways, and up higher at last to the throne.[4]

These are beautiful and comforting words, aren't they? But, dear one, with or without the emotional imagery, we have the sure promise of the presence of God's goodness and mercy...all the days of our life. Life is made up of "days," and God will be there at the dawn, the noonday, the evening, and through the dark night of each and every one of those "days." When you need His strength for your life's work each day, God will be there, extending to you all of His goodness and mercy. When you need His support for life's trials, when your green pastures become the dark valley of death, then, too, you can hold tightly to the hope of the promise of God's goodness and mercy. And when it is time for you to step across the threshold into the unknown, into "the house of the LORD," God's goodness and mercy will escort and follow you there, too. *Surely!!!!!*

What a marvelous promise of hope.

And now...let's at least *look* across that threshold into the unknown, into "the house of the LORD." Read on...

# ~12~

# God's Promise
# of Home

~

*And I will dwell in the house of the LORD forever.*
PSALM 23:6

*In My Father's house are many mansions;*
*if it were not so, I would have told you.*
*I go to prepare a place for you…*
*that where I am, there you may be also.*
JOHN 14:2-3

~

God's care for us all along the way
and His promise to care for us all the days of our life
are like fireworks—thrilling, exciting, brilliant.
But a home in heaven? An eternal home?
A place in the house of the Lord…forever?
Now *that's* like looking at the blazing heavens
after the flashes of fireworks fade away!
—*Elizabeth George*

*I*n the previous chapter, I mentioned the spectacle of fireworks so many people enjoy each Fourth of July. The finales of those expensive displays are electrifying, aren't they? But better yet is that wonderful moment after the finale, when the smoke from the gunpowder that ignites the splendid sprays and deafening booms clears away and you're left gazing at the solid splendor of the heavens. Oh yes, fireworks are stirring...but they're also momentary and man-made. But the heavens? God's moon and stars? Oh! The heavens declare His glory! They are the revealed handiwork of the Lord (Psalm 19:1)! They are stable and real, not merely loud blasts and puffs of smoke.

And, dear one, in this final verse of Psalm 23, David turns us away from this life—which the Bible calls "a puff of smoke," "a vapor that appears for a little time and then vanishes away" (James 4:14). He forces our gaze upward to heaven as he pronounces, "*And I will dwell in the house of the LORD forever.*" And, suddenly, as he speaks of our forever-home in the house of the Lord, the things of this world grow strangely dim as we're allowed a glimpse into the glory of heaven!

Well, my friend, God's care for us all along the way and His promise to care for us all the days of our life are like fireworks—thrilling, exciting, brilliant. But a home in heaven? An eternal home? A place in the house of the Lord...forever? Now *that's* like looking at the blazing heavens after the flashes of fireworks fade away! You see, God's promise of a forever-home is an eternal promise...and His most dazzling promise of all!

## Seven Reasons for Hope in the Future—Part II

And now, onward...and upward! Let's finish our "photo tour" we began in our last chapter of the cavernous depths of Psalm 23:6. So far on our tour of "Seven Reasons for Hope in the Future," we've seen these in Psalm 23, verse 6:

1) God's continued *goodness*   3) God's continued *pursuit*
2) God's continued *mercy*      4) God's continued *presence*

Having been escorted through *all the days of our life* by God's goodness and mercy, pursuit and presence, we finally reach the Father's house. At last we step into our eternal dwelling place. We are home at last!

## 5. Eternal Worship

Oh, how David—the shepherd, warrior, and fugitive—longs to be near God! To *dwell* with God *in the house of the Lord* was the paramount desire of his heart. He wants much more than merely being a guest in a tent along the way. He yearns to "dwell" with God and to be His forever-guest, not just an acquaintance or visitor for a brief stay. No, David wants to live with God. He wants to stay with Him. He wants to experience the fullness of joy and the forevermore pleasures of the Lord's presence!

And what will it be like to dwell in the house of the Lord forever? It will be to worship the Lord of that house...forever. Just as the Levites (who were assigned to serve the Lord in His sanctuary) considered the courts of the Lord to be their true home, David, too, has set his mind and heart there... ...for then he will be in the house of the Lord forever...where he will worship the Lord forever.

∾ ✻ ∾

## ∾ Reflecting on God's Promises ∾

Dear one, David is expressing himself and his thoughts in Psalm 23. Words are clues, and the words David chooses here in verse six communicate pure worship! He speaks from his heart to ours and tells us what is important to him. David, the poet, is letting us know exactly what consumes his heart and soul and mind... and it's the Lord. In fact, he's preoccupied *with* God. His passion is *for* God. His focus is *on* God. And his gaze is ever upward...to that place where he will one day dwell with God and worship Him forever.

David's upward gaze produced the Twenty-third Psalm, "the Pearl of the Psalms." We definitely know where his gaze was fixed. But, beloved, a better question is, "Where is *your* gaze fixed?" And what is it producing?

I found the musings of this writer a little too close to home! His "gaze" produced...

### The Twenty-third Channel

The TV is my shepherd. My spiritual growth shall want. It maketh me to sit down and do nothing for its name's sake, because it requireth all my spare time. It keepeth me from doing my duty as a Christian, because it presenteth so many good shows that I must see.

It restoreth my knowledge of the things of the world, and keepeth me from the study of God's Word. It leadeth me in the paths of failing to attend the evening church services, and doing nothing in the kingdom of God.

Yea, though I live to be a hundred, I shall keep viewing my TV as long as it will work, for it is my closest companion.

Its sounds and pictures, they comfort me.

It presenteth entertainment before me and keepeth me from doing important things with my family. It fills my head with ideas which differ from those in the Word of God.

Surely, no good thing will come out of my life because of so many wasted hours, and I shall dwell in my regrets and remorse forever.[1]

> As I asked before, where is *your* gaze fixed, my friend? What do you talk about? Where does your heart dwell? What is your greatest pleasure? The next time you hear yourself chattering on and on about a TV program, or the news, or the latest "talk" from a talk show, remember...your heart is showing! Turn *off* the Twenty-third Channel...and worship instead! Then you'll find yourself expressing praises like David did as he thought about the Lord...and worshiped.

## 6. *An Eternal Home*

Home. *The house of the Lord.* The concept of a house and a home has a deeply emotional effect on the heart of every person alive. But imagine what it meant to David. David, the shepherd, knew all about the nomadic life. Shepherds were on the move their whole life long, regularly pitching and moving their tents as they grazed their sheep. To have a house and a home was usually an unfulfilled dream for a shepherd.

David's whole life had been a pilgrimage, a journey home. He'd traveled through many a fair meadow and many a dark valley of death. He'd had his share of storms and adversaries. And God, the Shepherd, had never failed to care for him.

But David was ready for his troubled trek to end. He was ready to go home!

What did David mean by "the house of the LORD"? We know it couldn't have been the temple in Jerusalem, because it wasn't yet built. And it wasn't the house David wished to build for the Lord, because he used the word "forever" and no man-made house lasts forever.

No, it was something far greater than a house or a temple. It was another *life!* It was an eternal home. It was forever-fellowship with Jehovah beyond the grave. David was a king—and a wealthy one at that. And David possessed worldly riches and pleasures. But these worldly pleasures simply did not compare with the eternal pleasure of being at home in the house of the Lord...with the Lord of the house...forever.

∾ ✤ ∾

## ∾ *Reflecting on God's Promises* ∾

I well remember wrestling with my emotions when our daughter Katherine graduated from college and wanted to live in an apartment with a group of her college friends. " *Why?*" I fought! *"Why would she want to live with a group of girls when her home is only eight minutes away? What's wrong with our home?"*

But Katherine was 22 years old and her move seemed to be an obvious next step for her to take. So off she went to an environment which turned out to be a blessing—where she learned how to cook for others on a regular basis, to keep her part of the apartment clean, to enhance her side of the bedroom with her pretty little things, and to get along with others on a day-in-day-out basis.

But I'll also never forget Katherine's words the day she moved back home to prepare for her wedding. She sank into the sofa with a sigh and exhaled, "Mom, it's OK out there, but it's just not *home!*"

I think Katherine's sentiment is what David is telling us, dear one—"It's OK out there (in the world, in the marketplace, in our friendships, in our experiences, in managing our challenges)...but it's just not *home!*" We each yearn to be "no more a stranger or a guest, but like a child at home."[2] And that's what our forever-home means to us! May our hearts ever reflect this truth as we reflect with hope on the promise of our eternal home, on dwelling in the house of the Lord forever.

∽ ∽ ∽ ∽ ∽ ∽ ∽ ∽ ∽ ∽

# 7. *Eternal Presence*

There's no doubt that David broke some barrier when he penned the sentence, "*I will dwell in the house of the LORD forever.*" Reaching out with his heart toward the God whose eternal presence he so longed to enjoy, David reached out and touched a higher truth. As one has noted, "...there was something else beyond the sunset and evening star."[3] There was an eternal presence. There was God!

Just like David, you and I have conditions in our lives that make the promise of a forever-home in the presence of God something we look forward to. As we suffer here on earth—dealing with pain, affliction, deprivations, persecutions, and death—we, too, long to be in God's eternal presence there in the house of the Lord...*forever,* literally "to length of days"! Our earthly trials make the promise of heaven all the sweeter.

What awaits us there, dear one? What will we experience when we step across the threshold between earth and heaven? The writer of the book of Revelation tells us that God will be there. And He Himself will "wipe away every tear from [our] eyes; there shall be no more death, nor sorrow, nor crying; and there shall be no more pain" (21:4).

Imagine! No more tears, crying, sadness, enemies, trials, affliction, pain of heart, pain of body, wandering, climbing, trekking, and wading through life. All that we suffer will be removed...forever. And all that we yearn for will be provided...forever. What glory! What peace! Oh, what an existence it will be to dwell in the eternal presence of the Lord!

~ ✑ ~

### ~ *Reflecting on God's Promises* ~

The famous preacher D. L. Moody obviously thought much about stepping into the presence of God. He jotted these notes in the margin of his Bible beside Psalm 23:

For short sorrow, we shall have eternal joy.
For a little hunger, an eternal banquet.
For a little sickness and affliction,
    everlasting health and salvation.
For a little bondage, endless liberty.
For disgrace, glory.
For evil surroundings, the elect.
For Satan's temptations, the comfort of God.[4]

~ ~ ~ ~ ~ ✑ ~ ~ ~ ~ ~

I know our hearts hunger for the fulfillment of the promise of heaven, too. We long to worship the Lord...forever, to be at home with Him...forever, and to enjoy His presence...forever.

So, why don't we begin to worship Him and to enjoy His presence right here and now? On earth? Today...and every day? I know we're busy. Every woman is. And I know we're bombarded on every side with distractions and responsibilities. But, as David decided, "I have set the LORD always before me" (Psalm 16:8).

And what does it mean to set the Lord always before us? Read on...

∾ ✽, ∾

## ∾ *Reflecting on God's Promises* ∾

Some time ago, I read about a church youth leader who took her youth group on an outing to the Huntington Art Museum in Pasadena, California, to view the fine art treasures on display there. Once there, she intently whisked her group from room to room, from painting to painting, from display to display. She was determined that her group would see it all! But each time she crisscrossed the museum on the run, she caught sight of one particular room where a gentleman was seated on a bench across from one painting. While she and her brood were zipping through every nook and cranny of the vast museum, this man never moved. He remained on that bench for the entire time, drinking in the glory of one masterpiece.

With her goal of touring the museum and its legendary gardens accomplished, the church leader breathlessly bustled out of the museum to board the waiting bus with her group. And sure enough, as they left the grand hall, she caught sight of the man again. He was still there! As the bus bumped its way home after an exhausting day, she thought about that man. Yes, she concluded, his was the better way. Admitting that she could hardly recall what she had seen on her whirlwind tour, she could only imagine what that unknown man was taking home with him—the colors, the details, the understanding, the treasure, the appreciation, the comprehension, the feelings—of just one masterpiece.

∾ ∾ ∾ ∾ ∾ ❧ ∾ ∾ ∾ ∾ ∾

Why don't you and I, dear one, do what this wise man did? Why don't we set the busyness and bustle of life aside—at least for a time each day—and set the Lord before us? (Or, as one translator declares, "I keep the Eternal at all times before me.") Why don't we set the *many things* in life aside and enjoy the *One Thing*? Why don't we choose to sit and soak in His beauty, His essence, His majesty, His promises, and His glory...*now?*...*today?*

Beloved, when you and I make this daily decision to set the Lord before us, then we'll be able to join the writer who yearned for his promised home and wrote the heart-song of Psalm 84...

How lovely is Your tabernacle, O LORD of hosts!
My soul longs, yes, even faints for the courts of the LORD;
my heart and my flesh cry out for the living God.
(Psalm 84:1-2)

# A Final Reflection on God's Powerful Promises

One psalm. Six verses. Twelve powerful promises. One hundred and seventeen words. All truly awesome! I pray that you've thought much about all that God is and all that He promises—and does—for you. You, dear fellow traveler, shall not want anything...ever!

And now, before we leave these sacred words, I want to share with you one of my pastor's favorite stories about Psalm 23. It seems that in a church meeting one evening, the pastor had those who were visiting stand up and introduce themselves. The first to rise and give his name mentioned that he was an actor.

Thinking quickly, the pastor asked, "Do you know Psalm 23?"

"Why, yes," the actor replied with a smile.

"Would you mind treating our congregation to a recitation of it?"

"I would love to!" came his enthusiastic answer.

Rising in his place the artist turned, acknowledged his audience, cleared his throat, paused, and then launched into a flawless and eloquent oration of the familiar psalm.

When he finished, the people in the church burst into hearty applause. It was perfect! And such expression!

Before the pastor moved on to the next visitor, he thanked the actor and remarked, "It's obvious you know Psalm 23 well!"

The next gentleman to introduce himself as a visitor was an elderly senior, bent with age, who commented that he was a retired preacher.

"Oh! Then I'm sure you know Psalm 23, too!" exclaimed the pastor. "Why don't you share your rendition with our people."

With great difficulty the old man of God rose from his seat, turned, and with a raspy, aged, shaking voice, began. Slowly he articulated his way through the beloved psalm. More than once he had to stop and struggle with his tears. When he finally finished and sank into his seat, there was only the sound of choked sniffles as everyone sat, too stunned to move or respond.

Dabbing his eyes and finding his voice, the pastor of the church quietly spoke, "And you, sir, it's obvious that you know the Shepherd well."

∾∾∾∾∾

## A Final Prayer for You

As we go our separate ways, dear friend, my prayer for you is that you are now a woman who not only knows Psalm 23 well after we've walked through it together, but that you also know the Lord your Shepherd well. May you not merely appreciate the poetry and the imagery and the sentiments expressed in Psalm 23, but may you believe and abundantly experience God's powerful promises to you for each and every circumstance and season of life. As this poem reminds us,

> God is before me, He will be my guide;
> God is behind me, no ill can betide;
> God is beside me, to comfort and cheer;
> God is around me, so why should I fear?[1]

May you know full well and acknowledge with full confidence that "the Lord is my Shepherd."

# Notes

**God's Promises for You**

1. A. Naismith, *1200 Notes, Quotes, and Anecdotes* (London: Pickering & Inglis Ltd., 1975), 163.

2. Ray and Anne Ortlund, *The Best Half of Life* (Glendale, CA: Regal Books, 1976), 88.

3. Carole Mayhall, *From the Heart of a Woman* (Colorado Springs: Nav-Press, 1976), 10-11.

**Chapter 1—God's Promise of Care**

1. From the hymn "Come, Thou Fount of Every Blessing" by Robert Robinson.

2. Arnold A. Dallimore, *Susanna Wesley, the Mother of John and Charles Wesley* (Grand Rapids, MI: Baker Book House, 1994), 15.

**Chapter 2—God's Promise of Provision**

1. www.cbaonline.org/voice/back_list_main.htm—5/24/99.

2. A. Naismith, *A Treasury of Notes, Quotes, and Anecdotes* (Grand Rapids, MI: Baker Book House, 1976), 216.

3. *Life Application Bible—The Living Bible* (Wheaton, IL: Tyndale House Publishers, Inc., 1988), 42.

4. Curtis Vaughan, gen. ed., *The Old Testament Books of Poetry from 26 Translations* (Grand Rapids, MI: Zondervan Bible Publishers, 1973), 189.

5. G. Campbell Morgan, *Life Applications from Every Chapter of the Bible* (Grand Rapids, MI: Fleming H. Revell, 1994), 159.

**Chapter 3—God's Promise of Rest**

1. Albert M. Wells, Sr., ed., *Inspiring Quotations—Contemporary & Classical* (Nashville: Thomas Nelson Publishers, 1988), 15.

2. "Seven Minutes with God" from the ministry of the Navigators, Colorado Springs, CO.

3. Wells, *Inspiring Quotations*, 17.

4. W.G. Bowen, *Why! The Shepherd!* (c/o Mavis Bowen, Dansey Road, RD2, Rotorua, Nth Island, N.Z.), 30-31.

5. Vaughan, *The Old Testament Books of Poetry*, 189.

## Chapter 4—God's Promise of Peace

1. From the hymn "Like a River Glorious" by Frances R. Havergal.
2. From the hymn "Where He Leads Me" by E.W. Blandy and John S. Norris.

## Chapter 5—God's Promise of Healing

1. Information from Bowen, *Why! The Shepherd!*, 50-51.
2. Ibid., 52.
3. Ibid., 55.
4. H. Edwin Young, *The Lord Is...* (Nashville: Broadman Press, 1981), 36.

## Chapter 6—God's Promise of Guidance

1. Elizabeth George, *Beautiful in God's Eyes—The Treasures of the Proverbs 31 Woman* (Eugene, OR: Harvest House Publishers, 1998), 205.
2. Robert Alden, *Psalms—Songs of Devotion,* Vol. 1 (Chicago: Moody Press, 1974), 60.

## Chapter 7—God's Promise of Presence

1. Carole C. Carlson, *Corrie ten Boom: Her Life, Her Faith* (Old Tappan, NJ: Fleming H. Revell, 1983), 219.
2. Mrs. Charles E. Cowman, *Streams in the Desert,* Vol. 2 (Grand Rapids, MI: Zondervan Publishing House, 1966), 34.
3. Source unknown.
4. John Charles Pollock, *Hudson Taylor and Maria* (New York: McGraw-Hill, 1962), 206.
5. Source unknown.
6. Mrs. Howard Taylor, *John and Betty Stam—A Story of Triumph* (Chicago: Moody Press, 1982), 80.
7. Adapted from the song "Finally Home," author unknown.
8. Cowman, *Streams in the Desert,* Vol. 1 (Grand Rapids, MI: Zondervan Publishing House, 1965), 52.

## Chapter 8—God's Promise of Comfort

1. Herbert Lockyer, *All the Divine Names and Titles in the Bible* (Grand Rapids, MI: Zondervan Publishing House, 1980), 10.
2. F. B. Meyer, source unknown.
3. J. Allen Blair, *Living Reliantly—A Devotional Study of the 23rd Psalm* (Neptune, NJ: Loizeaux Brothers, 1980), 83.

## Chapter 9—God's Promise of Friendship

1. Naismith, *1200 Notes, Quotes, and Anecdotes,* 48.

2. M. R. DeHaan and Henry G. Bosch, *Our Daily Bread,* quoting H. W. Baker (Grand Rapids, MI: Zondervan Publishing House, 1982), January 26.

## Chapter 10—God's Promise of Protection

1. From the hymn "Like a River Glorious" by Frances R. Havergal.

## Chapter 11—God's Promise of Hope

1. Herbert Lockyer, *All the Promises of the Bible* (Grand Rapids, MI: Zondervan Publishing House, 1962), 10.

2. Curtis Vaughan, gen. ed., *The New Testament from 26 Translations—The New English Bible* (Grand Rapids, MI: Zondervan Publishing, 1967), 1161.

3. From the hymn "Great Is Thy Faithfulness" by Thomas O. Chisholm.

4. Alexander Maclaren, *Exposition of Holy Scripture, Psalms* (Grand Rapids, MI: Baker Book House, 1982), 103.

## Chapter 12—God's Promise of Home

1. Paul Lee Tan, *Encyclopedia of 7,700 Illustrations* (Winona Lake, IN: BMH Books, 1979), 1442-43.

2. Song lyric, source unknown.

3. Blaiklock, *Commentary on the Psalms,* Vol. 1 (Philadelphia: A.J. Holman Company, 1977), 63.

4. D. L. Moody, *Notes from My Bible and Thoughts from My Library* (Grand Rapids, MI: Baker Book House, 1979), 66.

## A Final Reflection on God's Promises

1. Source unknown.

# Bibliography

Alden, Robert. *Psalms—Songs of Devotion, Vol. 1.* Chicago, IL: Moody Press, 1974.

Arthur, Kay. *Lord, I Want to Know You.* Sisters, OR: Multnomah Books, 1992.

Blaiklock, E. M. *Commentary on the Psalms, Vol. 1.* Philadelphia, PA: A. J. Holman Company, 1977.

Blair, J. Allen. *Living Reliantly—A Devotional Study of the 23rd Psalm.* Neptune, NJ: Loizeaux Brothers, 1980.

Bowen, Walter Godfrey. *Why! the Shepherd!* (c/o Mavis Bowen, Dansey Rd., RD2, Rotorua, Nth Island, NZ).

Briscoe, Stuart. *What Works When Life Doesn't.* Wheaton, IL: Victor Books, 1976.

Cole, C. Donald. *Thirsting for God.* Wheaton, IL: Crossway Books, 1986.

Davis, John J. *The Perfect Shepherd.* Grand Rapids, MI: Baker Book House, 1979.

Jamieson, Robert, A. R. Fausset, and David Brown. *Commentary on the Whole Bible.* Grand Rapids, MI: Zondervan Publishing House, 1973.

Keller, Phillip. *A Shepherd Looks at Psalm 23.* Grand Rapids, MI: Zondervan Publishing House, 1979.

Kidner, Derek. *The Tyndale Old Testament Commentaries—Psalms 1–72.* Downers Grove, IL: InterVarsity Press, 1973.

Lewis, C. S. *Reflections on the Psalms.* New York: Harcourt Brace & Company, 1958.

Lockyer, Herbert. *All the Divine Names and Titles in the Bible.* Grand Rapids, MI: Zondervan Publishing House, 1980.

MacArthur, John. *The MacArthur Study Bible.* Nashville, TN: Word Bibles, 1997.

Meyer, F. B. *The Shepherd Psalm.* Fort Washington, PA: Christian Literature Crusade, 1973.

Pfeiffer, Charles F., and Everett F. Harrison. *The Wycliffe Bible Commentary.* Chicago: Moody Press, 1973.

Roper, David. *Psalm 23: The Song of a Passionate Heart.* Grand Rapids, MI: Discovery House Publishers, 1994.

Slemming, C. W. *He Leadeth Me.* Ft. Washington, PA: Christian Literature Crusade, 1977.

Spence, H. D. M., and Joseph S. Exell. *The Pulpit Commentary, Vol. 8.* Grand Rapids, MI: William B. Eerdmans Publishing Company, 1977.

Spurgeon, C. H. *The Treasury of David, Vol. 1.* Grand Rapids, MI: Zondervan Publishing House, 1950.

Stevenson, Herbert F. *Titles of the Triune God.* Old Tappan, NJ: Fleming H. Revell Company, 1956.

Stone, Nathan J. *Names of God.* Chicago, IL: Moody Press, 1944.

Unger, Merrill F. *Unger's Bible Dictionary.* Chicago, IL: Moody Press, 1972.

Wiersbe, Warren W. *Classic Sermons on the Names of God.* Grand Rapids, MI: Kregel Publications, 1993.

Young, H. Edwin. *The Lord Is...* Nashville, TN: Broadman Press, 1981.

# Personal Notes

# Personal Notes

# Personal Notes

# Personal Notes

# Personal Notes

# Personal Notes

# Personal Notes

# Personal Notes

# Personal Notes

# Personal Notes

# Personal Notes

# Personal Notes

~~~~~~ ✣ ~~~~~~

# Personal Notes

# Personal Notes

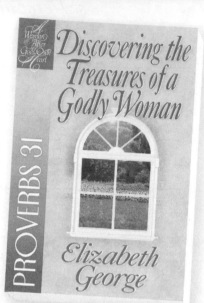

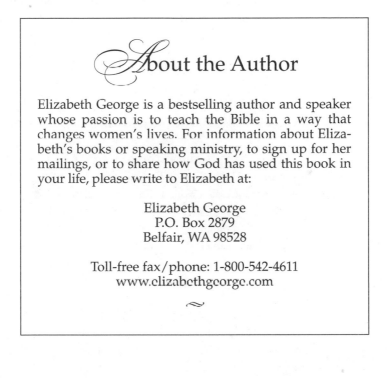

# $\mathscr{A}$bout the Author

Elizabeth George is a bestselling author and speaker whose passion is to teach the Bible in a way that changes women's lives. For information about Elizabeth's books or speaking ministry, to sign up for her mailings, or to share how God has used this book in your life, please write to Elizabeth at:

Elizabeth George
P.O. Box 2879
Belfair, WA 98528

Toll-free fax/phone: 1-800-542-4611
www.elizabethgeorge.com

## Books by Elizabeth George

Beautiful in God's Eyes—The Treasures of the Proverbs 31 Woman
Life Management for Busy Women
Loving God with All Your Mind
Powerful Promises™ for Every Woman—12 Life-Changing Truths from Psalm 23
A Woman After God's Own Heart®
A Woman After God's Own Heart® Deluxe Edition
A Woman After God's Own Heart® Audiobook
A Woman After God's Own Heart® Prayer Journal
A Woman's High Calling
A Woman's Walk with God
A Young Woman After God's Own Heart

### Growth and Study Guides

Life Management for Busy Women Growth & Study Guide
Powerful Promises™ for Every Woman Growth & Study Guide
A Woman After God's Own Heart® Growth & Study Guide
A Woman's High Calling Growth & Study Guide
A Woman's Walk with God Growth & Study Guide

### A Woman After God's Own Heart® Bible Study Series

Walking in God's Promises—The Life of Sarah
Cultivating a Life of Character—Judges/Ruth
Becoming a Woman of Beauty & Strength—Esther
Discovering the Treasures of a Godly Woman—Proverbs 31
Nurturing a Heart of Humility—The Life of Mary
Experiencing God's Peace—Philippians
Pursuing Godliness—1 Timothy
Growing in Wisdom & Faith—James
Putting On a Gentle & Quiet Spirit—1 Peter

### Children's Books

God's Wisdom for Little Girls—Virtues & Fun from Proverbs 31
God's Wisdom for Little Boys—Character-Building Fun from Proverbs
(co-authored by Jim George)